# THE REVITALIZATION OF SOUTHSIDE BAPTIST CHURCH

by Dr. Harry Fowler

Equip Press
Colorado Springs, Colorado

# THE REVITALIZATION OF SOUTHSIDE BAPTIST CHURCH

Introducing my ministry partner and wife of 55 years (2017), Beth Fowler. God has used her to encourage me and help bring out the best. She has literally followed me all around the world. She is also the mother of our two daughters. Beth, I love you with all my heart.

Dr. Harry Fowler

*Revitalization of Southside Baptist Church*
Copyright © 2018 by Dr. Harry Fowler
All rights reserved. No part of this publication may be reproduced, distributed, or transmitted in any form or by any means, without prior written permission.

Published by Equip Press, Colorado Springs, CO

Scripture quotations marked (ESV) are taken from *The ESV® Bible (The Holy Bible, English Standard Version®)* copyright © 2001 by Crossway, a publishing minis-try of Good News Publishers. ESV® Text Edition: 2011. The ESV® text has been reproduced in cooperation with and by permission of Good News Publishers. Unauthorized reproduction of this publication is prohibited. Used by permission. All rights reserved.

Scripture quotations marked (KJV) are taken from the King James Bible. Accessed on Bible Gateway at www.BibleGateway.com.

Scripture quotations marked (NASB) are taken from the New American Standard Bible® (NASB), copyright © 1960, 1962, 1963, 1968, 1971, 1972, 1973, 1975, 1977, 1995 by The Lockman Foundation, www.Lockman.org. Used by permission.

Scripture quotations marked (NIV) are taken from the *Holy Bible, New International Version*. Copyright © 1973, 1978, 1984, 2011 by Biblica, Inc.® Used by permission. All rights reserved worldwide.

Scripture quotations marked (NKJV) are taken from the *New King James Version®*. Copyright © 1982 by Thomas Nelson, Inc. Used by permission. All rights reserved.

Scripture quotations marked (NLT) are taken from the *Holy Bible, New Living Translation*, copyright © 1996, 2004, 2015 by Tyndale House Foundation. Used by permission of Tyndale House Publishers, Inc., Carol Stream, Illinois 60188. All rights reserved.

Scripture quotations marked (NRSV) are taken from the *New Revised Standard Version Bible*, copyright © 1989 the Division of Christian Education of the National Council of the Churches of Christ in the United States of America. Used by permission. All rights reserved.

First Edition 2018
Revitalization of Southside Baptist Church / Dr. Harry Fowler
Paperback ISBN: 978-1-946453-11-2
eBook ISBN: 978-1-946453-14-3

# DEDICATION

I WOULD LIKE TO DEDICATE THIS BOOK TO:
1. All the dedicated people at Southside who gave, served, and worked to make this dream possible.
2. All the people who had the dream of building a new church and died before seeing it happen.
3. To the Long Range Planning Committee for their tireless efforts in developing the meeting and planning process.
4. To all the new members who came after the relocation to help us reach the community for Christ and to strengthen our church.

# THE SOUTHSIDE STORY

**Introduction** — 9
**Foreword by Dr. Michael Cloer** — 13
**What Others Are Saying About the Southside Story** — 15

**STEP #1:** — 17
**The Southside Story, 1944-2009**
- 1944-1964 The Founding Years
- 1965-1985 The Glory Years
- 1986-1999 The Stable Years
- 2000-2009 Years of Conflict and Decline
- 2009–The New Leader Shows Up

**STEP #2:** — 23
**Understanding Church Dynamics**
- Identify Six Stages in the Church Life Cycle
- Identify 14 Growth Obstacles
- Identifying Terminal Diseases
- How Would You Describe Your Church?

**STEP #3:** — 33
**Gathering Data**
- Collecting and Analyzing Data
- Ministry Statistics 2000-2016
- Demographics of Five-Mile Radius
- Church Questionnaire
- Statistical Charts
- Growth Profile Summary
- 12 Recommendations

**STEP #4:** — 43
**Getting Ready, 2009-2012**
LONG-RANGE PLANNING
- Exploring the Finances
- Leap of Faith Campaign

**STEP #5:** — 49
**Moving Forward**
- Building the Initial Building
- The First Sunday and Beyond
- Problems to Resolve

**STEP #6:** — 57
**What's Next?**
- Assimilating New Members

**STEP #7:** — 61
**Moving Outward / Eight Outreach Ministries**
- Upward Soccer
- Turkey Shoot
- Operation Christmas Child
- Disaster Relief Ministry
- Handyman Ministries
- Bereavement Ministry
- Children and Youth Ministry
- Injoy Thrift Store

**STEP #8:** — 71
**Outward Special Events**
- Fall Festival
- Flashlight Easter Eggstravaganza
- Sports Sunday
- Shopping Events
- Biker Sunday

**STEP #9:** — 79
**Outward Missions**
- Local Missions
- State and National Missions
- International Missions
- Here Am I Lord, Send Me

**STEP #10:** — 83
**Getting Out The Word**
- The Church Newsletter
- How to Mail for Less Than Ten Cents Each
- Preparing the Mailout

**OUR CHURCH SPEAKS** — 92

**DEDICATION TO MIKE WALL** — 97

## Resources

**LEADING SOMEONE TO CHRIST**    100

**5 MOTIVATIONAL SERMONS**    101

**10 BIBLICAL GROWTH KEYS**    111

**WHAT EVERY PASTOR NEEDS TO KNOW ABOUT MILLENNIALS**    115

**THINGS I HAVE LEARNED ALONG THE WAY**    117

**CONCLUSIONS**    125

# INTRODUCTION

I love browsing through bookstores. Time easily gets away from me. Sometimes I buy something and sometimes I do not. Before I decide, I will pick up a book and glance through it.

**I ALWAYS ASK MYSELF FIVE QUESTIONS BEFORE BUYING A BOOK:**
1. Do I really need this book?
2. Can I do without this book?
3. Will this book help me in my ministry?
4. Is it worth the price?
5. Does the author know what he is talking about?

**CHURCH GROWTH EXPERTS AGREE:**
1. Ninety percent of all churches are declining.
2. Most churches reach their optimum size at 15 years of age.
3. Most churches have many obstacles and barriers to growth.
4. The longer a church stays the same size, the less likely it will grow.
5. The church on a serious decline is suffering from a DEATH SPIRAL.

**A QUICK CHECK UP**
Thom Rainer, president of Lifeway, recently wrote a Facebook article: "8 SIGNS YOUR CHURCH MAY BE CLOSING SOON." As I thought about these signs, I certainly agree with him.

**EIGHT REASONS YOU NEED THIS BOOK**
It is evident that many churches are on the precipice of closing. Read this checklist. If your church has FOUR OR MORE of these signs, it is likely that your church is on a death spiral and in deep trouble. Closing may be closer that anyone in the church realizes.

1. THERE HAS BEEN A NUMERICAL DECLINE FOR FOUR OR MORE YEARS. Worship attendance is in a steady decline. Offerings may decline more slowly as the "remnant" gives more to keep the church going. There are few or no conversions. Decline is clear and pervasive.
2. THE CHURCH DOES NOT LOOK LIKE THE COMMUNITY IN WHICH IT IS LOCATED. The community has changed its ethnic, racial, or socioeconomic makeup, but the church has not. Many members are driving from other places to come to the church. The community likely knows little or nothing about the church. And the church likely knows little or nothing about the community.
3. THE CONGREGATION IS MOSTLY COMPRISED OF SENIOR ADULTS. It is just a few years of funerals away from having no one left in the church.
4. FOCUS IS ON THE PAST AND NOT ON THE FUTURE. Most conversations are about "the good old days." Those good old days may have been 25 or more years in the past. Often a hero pastor of the past is held as the model to emulate. Planning sessions result in talking about what we did years ago in the good old days.
5. THE MEMBERS ARE INTENSELY PREFERENCE-DRIVEN. They are more concerned about their music style, their programs, their schedules, and their facilities than reaching people with the gospel. Their definition of discipleship is "others taking care of my needs." They want what they want and to keep things like they have always been.
6. THE BUDGET IS SEVERELY INWARDLY FOCUSED. Most of the funds are expended to keep the lights on and/or to meet the preferences of the members. There are few dollars for ministry and missions. And any dollars for missions rarely includes the involvement of the members in actually sharing the gospel themselves.

7. **THERE ARE SACRED COW FACILITIES.** It might be a parlor or a pulpit. It could be pews instead of chairs. It might be the worship center or the sanctuary. Members insist on holding tightly to those things God wants us to hold loosely.
8. **ANY TYPE OF CHANGE IS MET WITH FIERCE RESISTANCE.** The members are confronted with the choice to change or die. And though few would articulate it, their choice by their actions or lack of actions is the choice to die.

**CHECK THE OBSTACLES YOUR CHURCH IS FACING:**
- ☐ Numerical decline
- ☐ Decline in offerings
- ☐ Church does not look like the community in which it is located
- ☐ Decline in Baptisms
- ☐ Members are mostly senior adults
- ☐ The focus is on the past and not the future
- ☐ Budget inwardly focused
- ☐ Sacred cows
- ☐ Resistance to change
- ☐ We never did it that way before
- ☐ Few visitors

**Churches with three or more of these signs are closer to death than they realize.**

**THREE CHOICES OF A DECLINING CHURCH**

**CHOICE #1:** EMBARK ON A PROCESS OF CHANGE AND REVITALIZATION.

**CHOICE #2:** CLOSE THE DOORS for a season and re-open with a new name, a new vision, and some new people.

**CHOICE #3:** DO NOTHING—and you will CLOSE the doors forever.

**If you checked three or more items, you need this book.**

**WHAT PROMPTED ME TO WRITE THIS BOOK?**
1. Southside Baptist did not want to die.
2. This is a real story about the real people of Southside Baptist who took a leap of faith and experienced phenomenal growth as a result.
3. This book is filled with many ideas that led us to revitalization and turnaround.
4. This book is filled with testimonies and pictures of actual events.
5. If it can happen at Southside, it can happen anywhere.
6. This is not my story, but Southside's story
7. The church was willing to take a LEAP OF FAITH
8. I want to tell the whole world the what, how and when of the revitalization
9. My prayer is that you will be blessed and that YOU WILL EXPERIENCE REVITALIZATION
10. I believe God led me to write this book to be a blessing to many people.

DURING THE SEVEN YEARS FROM 2009-2016 we saw remarkable growth:
- Attendance last Sunday in old location **100**
- Attendance first Sunday in new location **305**
- Attendance my last Sunday **305**
- Total new members **305**
- Total baptisms **100**
- Worship average grew **75-225**
- Four Sundays' attendance exceeded **300+**

- Record attendance
  **327**
- Annual offerings grew from
  **$135,000 to $500,000**
- TOTAL 2016 MISSION GIFTS
  **$60,000**
- 2012: initial building seating capacity
  **215**
- 2013: added 200 additional seats—capacity
  **400**
- Fourteen classrooms, four restrooms, kitchen, two storage rooms, three offices, one lobby

**I WILL ATTEMPT TO TELL THE STORY OF HOW GOD BLESSED IN A SUPERNATURAL WAY. TO GOD BE THE GLORY!!!**

# FOREWORD BY DR. MICHAEL CLOER

Declining attendance, deteriorating buildings, dwindling resources, and discouraged members, all this causes one to ask, "I wonder if this church will ever recover?"

If you have ever thought that,(and many pastors and leaders have), then this book is a must read for you.

God used Dr. Harry Fowler to lead a Southern Baptist church in a downtown changing community to take intentional steps to refocus their goals, relocate their facilities, and revitalize their membership. In this book, he not only tells their story, but along the journey he stops frequently to draw observations and pass along valuable lessons that will greatly help any church in their journey to revitalization.

Writing it from a personal perspective, Pastor Harry allows the reader to not only gain valuable insight, but enjoy the stories, the candid remarks, and the humor of a seasoned, proven pastor.

I found it enjoyable, informative, challenging, and helpful for leaders in any size church. Pastors, deacons, teachers, young, old, experienced, and novices will all be glad they read this.


Michael Cloer, senior pastor
Englewood Baptist Church
Rocky Mount, North Carolina

# WHAT OTHERS ARE SAYING ABOUT THE SOUTHSIDE STORY

**REV. JOHN HAMM, Director of Missions, North Roanoke Baptist Association, Rocky Mount, NC**

Dr. Harry Fowler has many years of entrepreneurial experience in the area of church revitalization and served as a valuable ministry consultant for many churches. His passion for ministry and ability to love and relate well with people enables him to be a great encourager and inspirational motivator. He excels in the vital turn-around ministry skill of being able to analyze present circumstances and the willingness to patiently lead the church through a step- by-step vision toward a new future of effective ministry.

In this valuable book, Harry shares essential principles of church renewal ministry and specific practical ideas that were an integral part of the revitalization story of Southside Baptist Church. This resource will inspire you to think boldly and creatively, as you prayerfully discover the next steps in ministry for the congregation you serve.

**BILL BARKER, NAMB National Missionary, National Director of Appalachian Regional Ministry and the Mississippi River Ministry**

Harry has done it again. Thirty years ago, he wrote a book titled, "Breaking Barriers of New Church Growth: Increasing Attendance From 0-150." A simple book that enabled thousands of pastors and churches to experience new growth. It was a practical, hands on book written from the perspective of a practitioner and not from the ideology of a theorist. "The Revitalization of Southside Baptist Church," is a book on church revitalization written by a true practitioner, that walks a pastor and congregation through the process. While there are no magic formulas to revitalization, this book gives the essential principles and practices that any church can use in revitalization. It is a book I highly recommend to any church seeking revitalization.

**DR. CECIL JOHNSON, Founder and President Emeritus of Christian Bible College of Rocky Mount, Inc., Est. 1980**

I was extremely impressed as I read Dr. Harry Fowler's new book entitled "THE REVITALIZATION OF SOUTHSIDE BAPTIST CHURCH". It is a miraculous example of how God used Dr. Fowler and his leaders to totally turn around a dying church.

As you read his inspiring book, you will learn many "Church Growth Principles" in addition to other things which will help to increase the overall membership of your Church.

I think that the following scripture best describes how God used Dr. Fowler in his endeavors.
"A man's heart deviseth his way: but the Lord directed his steps." (Proverbs 16:9)

**MACK PEARSALL, entrepreneur, businessman, and lawyer**

*The Revitalization of Southside Baptist Church* by Pastor Harry Fowler is very inspiring, pragmatic, filled-with-humor, and has sound implemental advice that is applicable to building not only a church, but a business or any type of service organization. I could see and feel God's presence in the writer and in those dutiful souls who wisely chose to follow Pastor Harry's God-given sage advice and counsel and accomplished the miracle of revitalization.

**DR. ROBIN FISHER, pastor Sunset Ave Baptist, Rocky Mount, NC**

*The Revitalization of Southside Baptist Church* fills a needed niche in Kingdom work and "Revitalization". This book will be helpful to many churches as we try to rescue and relaunch dead and dying churches. This book is a great successful model.

# STEP #1: THE SOUTHSIDE STORY, 1944-2009

## UNDERSTANDING THE SOUTHSIDE STORY

1. WHEN GOD SHOWS UP THINGS HAPPEN
2. SOUTHSIDE WAS DOWN BUT NOT OUT
3. I WAS AT THE RIGHT PLACE AT THE RIGHT TIME
4. GOD USED ME AND MY SPIRITUAL GIFTS
5. GOD WAS READY TO HONOR THE FAITHFULNESS OF THE PEOPLE
6. THE FUTURE LOOKED BLEAK
7. GOD PERFORMED A MIRACLE

## 1944-1964

### THE FOUNDING YEARS

SOUTHSIDE was founded in 1944 in South Rocky Mount. The founding years of a church are always exciting. People look forward from Sunday to Sunday to see who will show up. God blessed us in many ways during this time. It is interesting to read and hear about the early stages, first starting with the Sunday school meeting in a chicken coop, building the education building, and later adding the sanctuary.

**Curtis Todd**, church member, was a general contractor and built the church. Hundreds of people lived around the church. Many lived within walking distance. The population around the church was primarily a blue-collar, hard-working people, with many railroad employees and retirees. The people took pride in what they built and were very committed to the Lord. The church grew numerically and spiritually. The foundations of how to do church were laid. The constitution and bylaws were developed. A good leadership foundation was laid and grew.

### CHURCH ADOPTED THE MOTTO "A LITTLE CHURCH WITH A BIG HEART."

This was pretty much the motto until 2012. The church developed a love and friendliness toward each other and welcomed visitors. The church is not little anymore. We outgrew the motto.

## 1965-1985

### THE GLORY YEARS

When asking long-time members when the church's best times were, almost all identified the GLORY DAYS when REV. LAWRENCE EVANS was pastor. He served 20 years from 1965-1985 and retired in 1985. No other pastor has served that long. Dr. Fowler had the second longest tenure, serving seven years.

Everyone loved Pastor Evans. He was a great pastor and preacher. It was obvious that he loved the Lord and the people. If someone was sick and in the hospital or sick at home, he was known to have sat all night with the family. After retiring, he served several area churches as interim pastor. He went to be with the Lord in 2009.

I knew Pastor Evans personally as I was pastor of Oakdale Baptist Church in Rocky Mount during some of the same years. We attended a SBC convention together in Dallas, Texas. He was a great friend to me.

When a pastor has a long tenure, his successor usually has a difficult time. No one can do anything like #1. This is not always the case but very often is the case.

These years were generally conflict free. The church experienced solid growth in new members, finances, baptisms, and attendance.

## 1986-1999

### THE STABLE YEARS

Toward the end of these years, the idea of relocation began to grow. There was a strong emotional tie to the current building and neighborhood. Some of the members who BUILT the church did not want to move and leave. The leaders looked for land and could not find a suitable place to relocate.

**Pastor Kenneth Cobb** served as pastor from 1993 to 1999. Pastor Ken saw that our current site of 21.4 acres out on NC 97 about 10 miles from the current location was for sale. Before Southside could take any action, another church purchased the property. Pastor Ken stopped and prayed over the land and claimed it for SOUTHSIDE. Pastor Ken had a great ministry at Southside and saw worship attendance grow from 65 to 132 and Sunday school attendance grow from 65 to 110.

The church responded to Pastor Ken's preaching and visiting and the church started growing. Under Pastor Ken's leadership a nursery was redone, a softball team was organized, and visitors started coming. Early in 1999, Pastor Ken felt he had done what he came to do and he moved to another pastorate.

**Secretary Becky Owens** served as church secretary from 1992 to 2000 and from 2002 to 2012. Many of those years were as a volunteer. Becky developed a food ministry and gave away food to many needy people. She did what she could. THANK YOU, BECKY, for the vital part you played during these years.

## 2000-2009

### YEARS OF CONFLICT AND DECLINE

These years were filled with turmoil. During these ten years there were five pastors and five interims. Three of the five pastors left under stress.

The church grew rapidly under Rev. Paul Gotthard. While he was pastor, he took about 100 people and attempted to start a new church. The effort later dissolved. He seemed to cater to people under 50 years of age. Many grown children of current members left with him and some went to other places never to return. A few eventually returned. This departure cut attendance in half.

---

Growth Key:
SHORT-TERM PASTORATES
HINDER CHURCH GROWTH.

---

## MOOD OF THE CHURCH 1999-2009

The leadership of the Long Range Planning Committee thought it would be a good idea not to relocate until the current facility could be sold. While this made a lot of business sense, the church never sold. There were hopes of building a church debt free. The tax value of the Church Street property was $1.25 million. The church had hoped to get at least one million dollars from the sale of the building. An offer of $650,000 was rejected. Later in 2012, the church sold for $400,000. The church split in 2002. In December of 2002, plans were presented to church members but they were unable to move forward. Land was quickly paid in full in spite of losing over half of the members. **SOME WHO LEFT WERE SAYING SOUTHSIDE WOULD NEVER PAY FOR THE LAND. BUT IT DID. LATER THEY SAID SOUTHSIDE WOULD NEVER RELOCATE BUT IT DID**. The land was paid for in June 2003.

In 2004, under the leadership of REV. TOM HALL, the church had the BRIDGE TO TOMORROW campaign at NC Wesleyan College. Monies raised at this event would go in the building fund to help fund the relocation project.

NONE OF THE PASTORS were able to lead the church to relocate. Ministry events were conducted on the new property. THE DREAM lived on in the hearts of many people. One of the biggest accomplishments during this decade, was paying for the land in 2003 ($225,000) after just a few years.

Attendance continued to dwindle. During these years there were a number of deaths. Some members became discouraged and moved on to other churches. Several interim pastors were well loved. Rev. Bill Tyndall and Dr. Doug Proffit, who served twice, and Dr. John Pepper were well liked and loved. Dr. Fowler began as interim but became pastor after a few months.

AROUND 2005, A NEW LONG RANGE PLANNING COMMITTEE WAS ELECTED (LRPC). *Jerry Reams served as chairperson, while Cecil Reams, Terry Tyson, Pam Jackson, Debbie Parker,* and *Grace Wallace* were elected to explore all possibilities. The committee wanted to make plans to relocate to the HWY 97 property.

Through all the problems, the DREAM never died.

---

Ecclesiastes 3:1-3 (KJV)
To every *thing there* is a season, and a time to every purpose under the heaven: A time to be born, and a time to die; a time to plant, and a time to pluck up *that which is* planted; A time to kill, and a time to heal; a time to break down, and a time to build up.

---

SOUTHSIDE had to go through a healing time before she could reach the building-up time. Many negative members left. The remnant never gave up. Other families left because they thought there was nothing for their young children and teens.

## SUMMARY, 2000-2009
- People had hoped to sell the old building for enough to pay for the new building.
- Exodus of many faithful teachers, deacons, tithers, and leaders weakened the leadership base.
- Five short-term pastorates in ten years crippled all forward progress. None of the five pastors were able to lead relocation efforts.
- There was an exodus of families with children.
- A New Long-Range Planning Committee was elected.
- In spite of the exodus, the church PAID FOR THE PROPERTY IN FULL!
- People realized the church was on a downward death spiral.
- For the most part, pastoral leadership was very ineffective.

## THE SITUATION WAS CRITICAL.
- The people did not want to quit.
- They did not want to give up.
- They had a mind to work.
- They wanted to relocate.
- Another bad experience with a pastor might well drive the last nail into the casket.
- The church did not know what to do.
- They prayed and depended on the Lord to send a leader.

## END OF 2000-2009 ERA
GOD WAS PREPARING HIS PEOPLE FOR
- A NEW DAY
- A NEW LEADER
- A NEW CHALLENGE
- MANY NEW OPPORTUNITIES

GOD WAS PREPARING A NEW LEADER FOR THE SOUTHSIDE CHALLENGE.

GOD'S TIMING IS ALWAYS PERFECT.
- GOD IS AN ON-TIME GOD
- GOD MOVED IN THE PEOPLE'S HEARTS
- PEOPLE PRAYED AND GOD HEARD THEIR PRAYER

## 2009: THE NEW LEADER SHOWS UP
It is always exciting to see who the next leader will be. It's a matter of timing and waiting for God to send the right person. Often, we hear of pastor search committees receiving upward of 200 resumes. Churches REVIEW each resume and often ask the church, "What traits do we want in the next pastor? What age? Education? Experience? What should he look like?"

At the time, I had just retired from YOUTH ON MISSION. I had three earned degrees, 44 years of ministry experience, was 66 years old, and was mostly bald and chubby. My wife of 48 years will tell you I am really good looking. At 66, I would be the oldest pastor the church ever had. Jim Joyner asked me to come for two Sundays. I agreed. AND THE STORY CONTINUES.

## DID I REALLY WANT TO GO TO SOUTHSIDE? I DID SOME RESEARCH.
I visited with Rev John Hamm, director of missions for the North Roanoke Baptist Association.

He shared with me some of the recent history of SOUTHSIDE. In the ten previous years, they had five pastors and five interims. Most of these years were very troubling.
- The church had one problem after another.
- One pastor ran into difficulty when it was discovered that his doctrine was not compatible with Southern Baptists. He left.
- The pastor just prior to my coming lasted eight months. His leadership style was more compatible with a military general. He fired the deacons and caused havoc in the church. The church fired him.
- What a history! As I discovered, there are two sides to every story. Several of the pastors were ineffective. Several were just in the wrong place at the wrong time and were not good matches.

ASKED SEVERAL PASTORS in the area, "What would you do? Would you go preach? What advice would you give me?"
- All but two gave me a negative response.
- Some said the church had no potential.
- Some said they were in a bad location.
- One person to whom I talked was Dr. Wendy Edwards. She was on staff at Southside in the mid 70s. Later she went to work with New River Baptist Association and later the NC Baptist State Convention.

WENDY EDWARDS told me that SOUTHSIDE really needed me. She said they were a real loving group. She strongly encouraged me to seriously pray about it. Wendy saw real potential.

With a mixed revue skewed toward the negative, I told Jim Joyner I would come for two Sundays. After the second Sunday, Jim asked me about being the interim. MY RESPONSE: I WILL LET YOU KNOW BY THE END OF DECEMBER. This would give me six weeks to see if the Lord was calling me.

## WHAT I FOUND PREACHING THESE SIX SUNDAYS NOVEMBER 15 – DECEMBER 31

I sensed a real need among the folks. I had worked with several troubled churches in the past. Several had dismissed their pastor just prior to my coming. I knew firsthand some of the dynamics they were facing. Working in the shadows of a long-term pastor may cause problems. But in my case it was a big blessing.

## I FOUND A REMNANT.
- I saw a group of people who were very discouraged.
- Some were discouraged because family members had left.
- FACT: If the next pastor was a bad experience, the doors might CLOSE FOREVER.
- I sensed a good number of people WHO were not ready to give up.
- I sensed a good number of people WHO wanted the church to TURN AROUND and be REVITALIZED.

**A WORD ABOUT FINANCES:** The deacons asked me about serving part time. They told me what they could pay. A compliment for the deacons: they did all they could and apologized for not being able to do more. God had provided me and Beth with some resources. Adding these resources to what the church could pay was just what we needed.

---

A word to ministers who might be reading my book:
Had I refused to pastor Southside because of the salary, I would have missed out on one of the greatest blessings of my life.

---

**ABOUT WORKING PART TIME:** I don't believe there is a part-time church. I jumped in and began visiting all the people; visiting the few visitors who came, which were few in the beginning; and visiting those in the hospital and the homebound. Soon attendance started increasing.

Knowing that I would never be #1 in the minds of many people, I did not even try. One day I received the biggest compliment from Donna, Brother Lawrence's daughter. She told me I was so much like her daddy. The way I preached and the way I did things. She went on to say that she believed that I did not preach for the money. I later had the privilege of preaching Brother Evans' widow's and Donna's mother's funeral, Mrs. Joyce Evans.

> **THREE BASIC PRINCIPLES FOR SUCCESS**
> 1. **LOVE** on the people and they **WILL** love **YOU** back.
> 2. **PREACH** the uncompromising, infallible **WORD** of **GOD**.
> 3. **GOD'S WORD WILL NOT RETURN VOID.**

## MY APPROACH TO BEING PASTOR

- I spent much time visiting and getting to know the people.
- I preached that the *Word of God is True and without error.*

## MY DRESS

- From April to October I usually wore a solid Hawaiian shirt.
- From November to March I wore long-sleeved shirts without a sport coat.
- LORD'S SUPPER and FUNERALS—I would always wear a coat and tie.

I found that my casual dress relaxed the crowd to come dressed comfortably. Younger people were not in the coat and tie scene.

It took some of our older people a little time to get used to my dress. One lady in particular would always come up to me and tell me how nice I would look if I had on a coat and tie. I would always explain why I did not wear a coat and tie. When I saw her coming I would know what she would ask me. And she knew my response. After a while, most of the men stopped wearing coats and ties.

## I ACCEPTED THEM LIKE THEY WERE. THEY ACCEPTED ME LIKE I WAS.

BOTTOM LINE: I HAD SEVEN HAPPY AND WONDERFUL YEARS AS PASTOR! I CRIED LIKE A BABY WHEN I LEFT AND HAVE CRIED MANY TIMES SINCE.

# STEP #2: UNDERSTANDING CHURCH DYNAMICS

**UNDERSTANDING CHURCH DYNAMICS** is important before you can understand how to do a church profile.

You need to be knowledgeable of the six stages in the life cycle and fourteen obstacles.

## Step #1: Identify Six Stages In the Church Life Cycle

*Research done by the Kairos Legacy* Partners states that every church will travel through FIVE natural stages of life with the SIXTH being DEATH. Applying dates to the stages, Southside's life cycle looks like this.

| STAGE #1 | Birth | 1944-1950 |
| STAGE #2 | Growth | 1951-1964 |
| STAGE #3 | Maturity | 1965-1985 |
| STAGE #4 | Plateau | 1986-1999 |
| STAGE #5 | Decline | 2000-2009 |
| STAGE #6 | DEATH | |

### STAGE #1: BIRTH STAGE

The people in the church usually get real excited when first starting OR restarting. You never know who will show up and how quickly you will grow. Important issues in this stage:
- Secure a meeting place— usually hotel meeting room or school
- Staffing: Minister and Worship Leader
- Leadership Team to oversee finances and ministry
- Develop budget
- Secure hymnals or projection equipment, keyboard
- Develop follow-up strategy
- Build database of visitors and attenders
- Set service times and frequency

### STAGE #2: GROWTH STAGE

Research shows that most churches reach their optimal size by year 15. A number of factors dictate this:
- Size of facility—attendance will not exceed 80 percent on a regular basis.
- Pastor's leadership style—micro or macro manager.
- Ability to retain visitors—depends upon follow up.
- Ability to assimilate new members into the body. Your church needs to become my church.
- Church usually constitutes and develops constitution and bylaws.
- Single cell and single fellowship church. More said about obstacles and barriers to growth in STEP #3.
- Leadership.
- By the end of STAGE 2, the first permanent structure will be built.

### STAGE #3: MATURITY STAGE
- Ways of doing things evolves.
- Processes are usually defined.
- Churches reach their peak attendance within 15 years.
- Leaders become entrenched with their responsibilities. Do not want to share with newcomers.
- The church begins to develop an inward focus.
- The longer a church stays the same size, the less likely it is to grow.
- Over time ways of doing things stagnates and crystallizes.
- Status quo evolves—resistance to change.

### STAGE #4: PLATEAU STAGE
- In this stage a church holds their own in attendance and finances.
- Attendance often begins a slight downward decline.
- Desire to reach new people diminishes.
- Everything stagnates—attendance, ministry, and offerings.

## STAGE #5: DECLINING STAGE
- Stage 5 comes just before death.
- Attendance and finances may drop gradually or drastically.
- Members talk about the possibility of closing the door.
- They begin discussing alternatives.

## STAGE 6: DEATH STAGE
*SOUTHSIDE WAS IN STAGE 5.*
- Unable to pay full-time pastor.
- Finances digressed to survival mode.
- Unable to pay bills timely.
- Members discouraged.
- Morale gets lower and lower.
- Focus becomes inward versus outward.
- SURVIVAL becomes the issue.
- Emphasis upon building maintenance.
- Status quo becomes the norm.

## 2000-2009 TOOK A TOLL ON SOUTHSIDE— A CLASSIC STAGE 5
- Pastors came and left.
- People get excited.
- Excitement diminishes.
- Pastors leave in conflict.
- Problems and conflicts arose.
- Attendance and offerings decrease.
- Fear of closure grows.
- People leave for other churches.

## Step #2: Identify Growth Obstacles

### OBSTACLE #1: CHANGE
Change causes many problems. Music wars are a big factor. Some prefer traditional music while others prefer contemporary music. Some churches attempt to develop a blended service to satisfy all. Millennials mostly prefer contemporary music.

Sometimes visitors do not return because they do not like the music. WET BABIES are the only people who like change.

### OBSTACLE #2: INADEQUATE SEATING
It is often said that attendance will not exceed 80 percent of the seating capacity on a regular basis. Our first Sunday in the new building attendance was 305. Seating capacity was 225. We exceeded capacity by 36 percent. We had two overflow rooms where some could sit and watch the service on a monitor. We knew this was not acceptable in the long term, but it was the best we could do.

Soon we began to develop plans to enlarge the worship seating capacity to 400.

### OBSTACLE #3: RESTROOMS AND NURSERY
These two rooms are the most important rooms in the church. They both need to be clean, attractive both to the eye and nose. KEEP THESE ROOMS CLEAN AND WELL STOCKED WITH SUPPLIES.

### OBSTACLE #4: SURVIVAL
FINANCES allow little opportunity to pay extra staff and little money for ministry expenses. As the church ages, survival finances become the order of the day. There is little extra money. Only necessities are given attention.

### OBSTACLE #5: ENTRANCE POINTS
*WHAT IS AN ENTRANCE POINT?*
Think of it this way. What is happening at the church that attracts new people?

Everyone has these needs, including visitors.

Our Basic Needs
- The need to be cared for
- The need to be loved
- The need to be involved
- The need to belong

People find their way into a church through one or more entrance points. The larger the church, the more entrance points it has.

**ENTRANCE POINTS INCLUDE:**
- Pastor's ministry
- Friendliness of people
- Children's ministry
- Youth ministry
- Upward Sports
- Good music
- Special events
- Mission trips
- Teaching opportunities
- Small groups

The pastor and people are the first two entrance points. In addition to the pastor's ministry, people were attracted to Southside through the children and youth programs, Upwards Soccer, and special events.

## THE MORE ENTRANCE POINTS, THE MORE VISITORS.

### OBSTACLE #6: INWARD FOCUS

As a church ages, the focus tends to gravitate toward meeting the needs of those attending. Little attention is given to outreach AND visitor follow-up. Many people ride by the church every day. They are welcome if they want to come.

Research on the unchurched teaches that people WILL come if invited by someone. An inward-focused church makes no conscious outreach efforts. All events and ministries are focused on the members.

### OBSTACLE #7: PASTORAL LEADERSHIP

In my book *Breaking Barriers of New Church Growth*, I identified several numerical barriers that churches seem to gravitate toward: 35, 75, 125, and 200. Since my research dealt with the smaller church, I spent more time with the 35, 75, and 125 barriers. The North American Mission Board, Church Extension Department, works with church planters. Since most churches in the US are under 100 in attendance, the HMB asked me to write a book that would help these churches grow. A questionnaire was mailed to all the SBC church planters in the US asking them for certain information. I compiled the results in my book. A copy was given to all 1,000 church planters. Eleven colleges and seminaries used it as a textbook. I taught these principles on a mission trip to *South Africa, Botswana, and Zimbabwe and all over the United States*. Here are the results of my research and writing.

THE 35 ATTENDANCE CHURCH
- THE PASTOR IS A SHEPHERD.
- He knows his sheep by name.
- He becomes a family member to all families.
- He makes all the hospital visits.
- He's expected to visit in everyone's home.
- He attends anniversaries, birthdays.
- He may not be a real decision maker.
- Church has strong lay leadership.
- There are one or two adult Sunday school classes.
- Pastor tends to be a micro-manager.
- As church grows toward 75, the structural leadership base must enlarge.
- Church must expand number of decision makers. A small church usually has two or three decision makers. When a pastor leaves after a short tenure, the power of these three leaders becomes stronger.
- Decisions are not made in the deacons' meeting or church business meeting but rather in groups.
- Two or three head leaders tend to make the decisions. People have little say.

LYLE SCHALLER says that normally it takes five years for the pastor to become the leader. Most pastors do not stay that long and rarely become the leader.

### SOUTHSIDE EXPERIENCED RAPID PASTORAL CHANGE.
- One pastor's doctrine was inconsistent with Southern Baptist doctrine.
- One was not a good example and did things that caused the church to question him.
- Many younger families who grew up in the

church thought Southside would never build, never be anything for their children. They left for other churches and most never returned.
- Lack of good pastoral leadership creates division and discord.
- People interpreted their inability to move forward as GOD'S TIMING WAS NOT RIGHT.

In SOUTHSIDE'S situation, I became the leader overnight. Several factors allowed this dynamic to happen.
- Rev. Evans, the longtime pastor, and I were friends.
- The people realized their church was just about to close.
- They respected me as their leader.
- I had lived in Rocky Mount for 33 years and had a good reputation in the city.
- I had led a conference in Southside years earlier.
- I felt accepted from day one. They knew I was there to help them and not hurt them. I was 66 at the time. Sometimes older men do have an advantage.

---

The turnaround pastor
- He is a motivator.
- He is an encourager.
- He is a vision caster.
- He has the gift of faith.
- He is a team player.

---

## REASONS FOR DIFFICULTY
- Long-time leaders protect turf
- Social intimacy is preserved—we know everyone by name
- Leaders maintain control

## OBSTACLE #8: FACILITIES
Church growth research indicates that a church will not exceed 80 percent of its capacity. The building on Church Street had plenty of room for 300 for both education and worship space. The LRPC needed to keep this in mind when drawing plans for the new building. LACK OF WORSHIP AND EDUCATION SPACE was not an obstacle in the prior location.

---

The longer a church is the same size, the more difficult it is to grow beyond that size.

---

## OBSTACLE #9: WORSHIP STYLES
*THERE ARE NUMEROUS TYPES OF MUSIC:*
- Traditional
- Contemporary
- Blue Grass
- Southern Gospel

*PREACHING STYLES:*
- Teaching
- Preaching

Generally, younger people like a contemporary worship style and older people like a more traditional style.

Generally, the older people like the old hymns and the younger people like the praise songs. We tried to develop a blended service to include music of each type. Churches with two morning worship services usually have one contemporary service and one traditional. Others seek a blended service.

CHURCH VISITORS will make a judgment call when attending worship service—Are we coming back? The basic issue is, Do we like the music? Do we not like the music?

ANOTHER WORSHIP FACTOR is preaching style. At Southside, I included plenty of opportunities for our associate pastor to preach. He is a gifted teacher of the WORD. CJ needed experience so that he might grow as a preacher. He preached on Sunday nights and when I was away for whatever reason on Sunday mornings. I would ask him first if he would like to preach. Some people liked his style and some people liked my style. I thought we blended well together.

## OBSTACLE #10: LACK OF VISION

> Proverbs 29:18 (KJV)
> Where *there is* no vision, the people perish.

**CHURCHES DECLINE BECAUSE OF THE LACK OF VISION.**

In growing churches, the pastor is the vision caster.

In Nehemiah, the walls of the city were broken down. God called Nehemiah to lead the people in repairing the walls of Jerusalem.

> *Nehemiah 2:18 (KJV)*
> *Then I told them of the hand of my God which was good upon me; as also the king's words that he had spoken unto me. And they said, Let us rise up and build. So they strengthened their hands for this good work.*

The story goes that Nehemiah had received a vision from God. He developed a burden for rebuilding the wall. He knew he could not do this by himself. So to accomplish this project, he got a few good men to go and view the work to be done.

Once they had made the decision to rebuild the wall, all the resources were provided. The resources showed up after they made the decision to rebuild.

## OBSTACLE #11: CHURCH INFRASTRUCTURE

A church is made up of three units:
1. **CELL:** could vary from 5 to 15 people. Groups are very intimate, small face-to-face groups. Could be home groups or Sunday school classes.
2. **FELLOWSHIP GROUPS:** 15-75 people. Have regular large group activities; everyone knows everyone.
3. **CONGREGATION:** Total of all cells and fellowship groups.

**SOUTHSIDE INFRASTRUCTURE AFTER TURNAROUND**

FOUR ADULT FELLOWSHIP GROUPS:
- Older adults
- Middle-aged adults
- Young adults
- College students

AVERAGE ATTENDANCE: 225-250

## Identifying Terminal Diseases

TERMINAL DISEASES can be treated and slowed but not cured. Treatment can prolong life and sometimes the disease may go into remission but is seldom cured. A church can prolong death but must deal with terminal illnesses. Churches close their door every year because they are unable to make a TURNAROUND. We identified three TERMINAL DISEASES that plagued SOUTHSIDE: OBSTACLES 12, 13, AND 14.

## OBSTACLE #12: LOCATION

When Southside was originally ORGANIZED in 1944, South Rocky Mount was a thriving part of the city. The original church had a great location. Many people lived within walking distance. It was a safe place to live and raise your children. Houses were moderately priced. Churches in the area thrived and grew. South RM Church of God, Grace Free Will Baptist Church, and Southside were growing and thriving. As the years passed, the community experienced change. The community became multi-racial.

> Learning Nugget:
> Turning a stage 5 church around is difficult, if not impossible.
>
> Matthew 19:26 (KJV) says "but with God all things are possible."

Today, two black churches are growing and thriving in the neighborhood. Praise City bought Southside's building and has added 100 new members since moving. Greater Joy Baptist Church, a black church, bought South RM Church of God and is experiencing phenomenal growth. One church remains of the three—Grace Free Will. At one time they were one of the larger churches in the city and now attendance is 35-50.

As you drive around in the community, new property owners have done a good job maintaining their property. Normally in a changing community, property values drop, crime increases, and many whites move out. Property values, while they have not appreciated, have maintained their value.

On several occasions, Southside went door to door visiting and distributing information about the church, inviting people to come. This effort was repeated several times over the years. RESULTS: One person and his two children came. "And the lord said unto the servant, Go out into the highways and hedges, and compel them to come in, that my house may be filled" (Luke 14:23, KJV). While Southside obeyed this biblical command TO GO but there were few to no results.

SOUTHSIDE learned that a white church located in a predominantly black community is not attractive to black people.
- Worship styles, both music and preaching, are different.
- Customs and ethnic backgrounds are different.

One church has been successful in reaching the blacks by providing tutoring, food and clothes distribution, and social ministries.

METHODS that worked years ago do not work today. In the nineteenth century, circuit riding preachers were very successful. Charles Wesley would start Bible studies everywhere he traveled. These studies thrived and many came to salvation.

## One of today's challenges for church leaders is to work smarter and not harder.

I can remember in years past, churches had two revivals per year, one in the spring and one in the fall. Businesses would close and everyone went to the revival services. No stores were open on Sunday. Revivals would start on Sunday and go through to the next Sunday. Some lasted two weeks. I remember past revivals were well attended. In my younger years, I preached about six revivals per year. Revivals today are attended by the faithful few. Recently I talked to a full-time evangelist who has preached revivals for 30 years. He said it is getting harder and harder to fill his schedule because churches are just not having revivals.

## A Learning Nugget: A church can wait too long to relocate and reach a point they can't.

### OBSTACLE #13: OLD AGE
*OCCURS WHEN THE AVERAGE AGE OF PEOPLE IN THE CHURCH IS 60+*

It is difficult or impossible to attract young families when there are no young families in the church. Prospective families are looking for churches where they can involve their children.

Older leaders die and are not replaced with younger leaders. One of the blessings at Southside after moving to the new location was that we reached many young adults aged 20-35. The current youth leader is a young lady, a recent college graduate, and a first-year school teacher. She is doing a great job.

*OLD AGE IS A DIFFICULT OBSTACLE TO OVERCOME.*

A few years ago, a church asked me to come and do a church growth profile, looking at their past, present, and future. As I gathered information and did interviews, I discovered that 75 percent of the people were over 65. SBC research shows that 80 percent of all new members who join a church are children of current members.

I told the church there are three kinds of growth:
1. **BIOLOGICAL:** children of members,
2. **CONVERSION:** people won to the Lord and baptized,
3. **TRANSFERS:** people who move membership from another church.

## ISSUES OF A PREDOMINANTLY OLDER CHURCH:
- Youth and children's ministries are weak or non-existent.
- An older church does not attract younger couples with children.
- GROWTH becomes difficult or impossible.
- Adults talk more about the past than about the present or future.
- As older members die, they are not replaced.
- Attendance shrinks.
- Older members do not have the ENERGY to run a full ministry program.
- The church becomes an ANNIVERSARY church. They talk more about what used to be rather than what could be. The past is more glorious than the present or future.

Recently I preached in a church that once had 200 in attendance. They relocated, and through years of change, attendance declined. On this day, there were 25 people present. Of the 25, 20 were 70 and above. There were no children and no teens in the church. The church building is beautiful, fairly new, and well kept. They still have a building payment. Finances are insufficient to pay a full-time pastor. Without children, they cannot attract youth and children. With several funerals per year, and as finances decrease, their ability to grow is next to ZERO.

When churches reach this point, there are basically THREE choices:

1. MERGE WITH ANOTHER CHURCH,
2. CLOSE THE DOORS AND SELL THE CHURCH, OR
3. REPLANT AND REORGANIZE.

These are tough choices. No one wants to be a quitter. A few years ago, there was a church in our city that sold their building and gave the money in an endowment for missions. Their money goes on and on.

SOUTHSIDE HAD NOT YET REACHED THIS POINT BUT THEY WERE CLOSE. There were few families with children in the church. We read and hear about hundreds of churches that close their doors and many pastors leave the ministry for a variety of reasons every year.

For 11 years Southside had UPWARD SOCCER. In the earlier years before our church grew, the Upward director, Debbie Parker, asked, begged, pleaded for workers. I did the same from the pulpit. But to no avail. Most of the folks were just beyond the age they could run the soccer field. We had two choices:
- SEEK leadership outside the church or
- NOT have the program.

Debbie and the leadership team chose to seek leadership outside the church. Debbie and her team never gave up. Upward Soccer has been extremely successful.

I remember the first time I went in the nursery at Southside. You could tell it had not been used in some time. It was clean, pretty, and well equipped. But it was EMPTY—NO BABIES. These older members had raised their children in this nursery. They had worked hard in the church and community. There were many memories in the nursery and church. I could almost hear children crying and music playing Jesus Loves Me.

AN AGING MEMBERSHIP IS DIFFICULT TO OVERCOME. We are getting no younger.

Dr. Peter Wagner, church growth expert from Fuller Theological Seminary, calls OLD AGE a TERMINAL ILLNESS. Once the average age of the folks begins creeping above 60-65, age becomes an issue.

OUR OLDER ADULTS
- Were faithful in their attendance, tithes, and dedication.
- Were part of the GREATEST GENERATION.
- Never gave up their dream of relocating to the new community.

Many gave time and money to make relocation happen, but never saw the new church. They died before we realized the dream.

**STRENGTHS OF THE OLDER PEOPLE**
- THEY NEVER GAVE UP THEIR DREAM
- THEY DID THE BEST THEY COULD
- THEY GAVE, THEY GAVE, THEY GAVE
- THEY WERE LOVING AND KIND
- THEY HAD A STRONG COMMITMENT TO GOD
- THEY LOVED ME AND BETH
- THEY APPRECIATED OUR WORKING WITH THEM

**OBSTACLE #14: CONFLICTS**
*2000-2009 WAS FILLED WITH CONFLICTS THAT CENTERED AROUND THE PASTOR AND LEADERSHIP*
Churches do not grow in the midst of turmoil. During these ten years, moving forward was crippled.
- There were at least two strong interim pastors who served twice.
- One pastor had poor leadership skills and was dismissed.
- One pastor's doctrine was inconsistent with Southern Baptist doctrine.
- One was not a good example and did things that caused the church to question him.
- Many younger families who grew up in the church thought Southside would never build, never be anything for their children. They left for other churches and most never returned.
- Lack of good pastoral leadership creates division and discord.
- People interpreted their inability to move forward as GOD'S TIMING WAS NOT RIGHT.

As I write this assessment tears are rolling down my face. God often chooses an unlikely person to do unlikely things. I was willing to give it my best. I had NO building experience. But I did know how to love on the people.

Thought Questions:
In which stage is your church?

Stage #1: Birth
Stage #2: Growth
Stage #3: Maturity
Stage #4: Plateau
Stage #5: Decline
Stage #6: *Death*

Which obstacles are your church facing?

# HOW WOULD YOU DESCRIBE YOUR CHURCH?

___ A. FUTURE ORIENTED
___ B. PRESENT ORIENTED
___ C. PAST ORIENTED

___ A. DECISIONS BASED ON FAITH
___ B. DECISIONS BASED ON AVAILABLE RESOURCES
___ C. INDECISION

___ A. VISION DRIVEN
___ B. PROGRAM DRIVEN
___ C. STRUCTURE DRIVEN

___ A. INVESTS FINANCES FOR MISSIONS
___ B. PROVIDES FINANCES FOR MINISTRY
___ C. PRESERVES FINANCES FOR MAINTENANCE

___ A. COMMUNITY FOCUSED
___ B. CONGREGATION FOCUSED
___ C. CORE GROUP FOCUSED

___ A. MEMBERS SERVE BASED ON SPIRITUAL GIFTS
___ B. MEMBERS SERVE BASED ON PROGRAMS OF THE CHURCH
___ C. MEMBERS SERVE BECAUSE NO ONE ELSE WILL DO IT

___ A. INNOVATIVE
___ B. ROUTINE
___ C. COMPLACENT

___ A. NEW LEADERSHIP
___ B. STAGNANT LEADERSHIP
___ C. ENTRENCHED LEADERSHIP

___ A. DEMONSTRATES HIGH RISK FAITH
___ B. DEMONSTRATES LOW RISK FAITH
___ C. DEMONSTRATES NO RISK FAITH

___ A. CONVERSION GROWTH
___ B. TRANSFER GROWTH
___ C. NO GROWTH

**Count Your A, B, C Answers:**

Your **A** correspond with **INCLINE**
Your **B** correspond with **RECLINE**
Your **C** correspond with **DECLINE**

Reprinted from *REVITALIZE*
Church Health and Revitalization Team
Brian Upshaw, NC Baptist Convention

# STEP #3: GATHERING DATA

## STEP #1: REFLECT ON THESE QUESTIONS
- What do you think God wants us to do?
- Are you willing to take a LEAP OF FAITH?
- Do you really believe NOTHING is impossible?
- Are you willing to make a three-year commitment that our church can move forward?

## STEP #2: ANSWER THESE QUESTIONS
1. When were the glory days of the church?
2. What do the statistics show us?
3. What were the major accomplishments?
4. Has there been any new construction during this time?
5. What is the average age of the members?
6. What is the number and ages of the children?
7. CHART TOTAL OFFERINGS—Have they increased?
8. CHART THE STATISTICS—Is the church growing, plateaued, or declining?

## STEP #3: STUDY LIVING PATTERNS
On a map, chart where the members, regular attendees, and visitors live. This will be helpful in planning future outreaches.

## STEP #4: INTERVIEW 15-25 MEMBERS
Choose a variety of members with various lengths of membership who are both young and old. Interview 15-25 members. Ask them these questions:
- When were the BEST DAYS of the church? What happened then?
- When were the WORST days?
- What are several major events you remember?
- What would you like to see the church do in the next five years?
- What are your church's biggest STRENGTHS?
- What are your church's biggest WEAKNESSES?

## STEP #5: STUDY DEMOGRAPHIC DATA
This study will tell you about ministry areas.
- Average age and age groups
- Education levels
- Income levels

## STEP #6: STUDY PAST 20-YEAR STATS
- Sunday school attendance.
- Worship attendance.
- Mission giving.
- Total tithes and offerings.
- New members.
- Baptisms.
- Usually 25 percent of people attend every Sunday.
- To average 200 in worship attendance, 250-275 must attend at least one Sunday per month.

## Collecting and Analyzing Data

*TO DEVELOP AN ACCURATE GROWTH PROFILE, YOU MUST COLLECT AND ANALYZE DATA.*

**Step #1:** Collect 15-20 Years' Worth Of Church Data
**Step #2:** Analyze Church Data
**Step #3:** Study Demographics
**Step #4:** Do Interviews
**Step #5:** Prepare Report With Recommendations

## STEP #1: COLLECT 15-20 YEARS' WORTH OF DATA
Southside results
- Categories increased 2000-2001
- Attendance dropped in half 2002-2005
- Slight growth 2005-2007
- Decline and plateau 2008-2011
- Rapid growth 2012-2016
- VBS grew 2012-2016
- Giving grew 2012-2016
- Baptisms grew 2012-2016

## STEP #2: ANALYZE CHURCH DATA
- Determine average age
- Plot living patterns
- STUDY THESE QUESTIONS
    - What would you like to see your church do in the next five years?

- In the next ten years?
- You will need to figure out how to capture attendance frequencies for this stat.
- What are the church's biggest strengths?
- What are the church's biggest weaknesses?
- What is your church known for? What have you wanted to tell pastor?

## STEP #3: ANALYZE DEMOGRAPHICS
POPULATION IS STABLE
- Slightly growing
- 6,500 households
- Mostly married couples
- High majority white
- Predominately college educated
- 2-1 white collar / blue collar ratio
- $72,000 upper annual income

### DEMOGRAPHICS OF NEW AREA
1. PROSPECTS AND VISITORS will be more white collar.
2. ASSIMILATION: How will we assimilate the old with the new?
3. MINISTRY TO SINGLES.
4. MINISTRY TO families living together. Do we accept them?
5. ARE NON-ANGLOS welcome? Are we prepared to accept people not like us?
6. ARE WE PREPARED TO MINISTER TO CHILDREN FROM DIFFERENT SCHOOLS? Public? Private? Home?

## STEP #4: DO CHURCH MEMBER INTERVIEWS

## STEP #5: PREPARE RECOMMENDATIONS AND REPORT

## MINISTRY STATISTICS 2000-2016

|      | AM Worship | Total Members | Sunday School | Total Receipts | Designated Receipts | VBS | Baptisms |
|------|-----------|---------------|---------------|----------------|---------------------|-----|----------|
| 2000 | 168 | 498 | 105 | 350,717 | 203,369 | 0 | 11 |
| 2001 | 170 | 503 | 90 | 346,735 | 243,457 | 47 | 22 |
| 2002 | 96 | 447 | 105 | 240,884 | 175,085 | 66 | 10 |
| 2003 | 97 | 446 | 81 | 194,578 | 143,443 | 68 | 5 |
| 2004 | 87 | 430 | 70 | 211,719 | 133,023 | 76 | 7 |
| 2005 | 103 | 432 | 80 | 209,091 | 139,633 | 50 | 4 |
| 2006 | 116 | 427 | 74 | 186,278 | 128,253 | 54 | 0 |
| 2007 | 114 | 417 | 74 | 177,100 | 139,623 | 60 | 0 |
| 2008 | 84 | 412 | 54 | 150,578 | 120,822 | 60 | 2 |
| 2009 | 80 | 403 | 61 | 142,518 | 116,292 | 0 | 1 |
| 2010 | 72 | 394 | 54 | 163,295 | 108,688 | 50 | 3 |
| 2011 | 80 | 402 | 90 | 168,617 | 118,869 | 96 | 8 |
| 2012 | 200 | 483 | 135 | 309,133 | 195,614 | 175 | 6 |
| 2013 | 213 | 546 | 128 | 653,650 | 297,587 | 256 | 15 |
| 2014 | 231 | 576 | 131 | 669,829 | 349,937 | 259 | 25 |
| 2015 | 254 | 591 | 122 | 484,496 | 324,284 | 193 | 7 |
| 2016 | 204 | 610 | 115 | 610,495 | 342,095 | 183 | 21 |

# DEMOGRAPHICS OF FIVE-MILE RADIUS

| YEAR | 2010 | 2016 | 2021 |
|---|---|---|---|
| POPULATION | 16,369 | 16,595 | 17,226 |
|  |  |  |  |
| CHANGE | 32.0% | 1.4% | 3.8% |

### NUMBER OF HOUSEHOLDS

| 2000 | 2010 | 2016 | 2021 |
|---|---|---|---|
| 4,869 | 6,430 | 6,518 | 6,763 |
|  | 32.1% | 1.4% | 3.8% |

### FAMILY WITH CHILDREN

|  | 2010 | 2016 | 2021 |
|---|---|---|---|
| MARRIED COUPLES | 1,031 | 1,385 | 1,334 |
| SINGLE MOM | 641 | 394 | 402 |
| SINGLE DAD | 180 | 141 | 161 |

### AGES

| AGES | 2010 | 2016 | 2021 |
|---|---|---|---|
| 0-4 | 959 | 961 | 938 |
| 5-17 | 2,923 | 2,652 | 2,562 |
| 18-24 | 1,120 | 1,559 | 1,621 |
| 25-34 | 1,717 | 1,603 | 1,954 |
| 35-54 | 4,878 | 4,365 | 4,004 |
| 55-64 | 2,431 | 2,479 | 2,517 |
| 65+ | 2,341 | 2,975 | 3,579 |

| WHITE COLLAR | **65.1%** |
|---|---|
| BLUE COLLAR | **34.9%** |

### POVERTY LEVEL

| ABOVE POVERTY | 4,355 (92.3%) |
|---|---|
| BELOW POVERTY | 364 (7.7%) |

### EDUCATION LEVEL

|  | 2016 | 2021 |
|---|---|---|
| LESS THAN 9TH GRADE | 433 | 435 |
| SOME HS | 871 | 851 |
| HS GRAD | 3,517 | 3,552 |
| SOME COLLEGE | 2,616 | 2,791 |
| ASSOCIATES DEG | 1,068 | 1,161 |
| BACHELORS DEG | 2,046 | 2,281 |
| GRADUATE + | 872 | 985 |

### HOUSEHOLD INCOME

|  | 2010 | 2016 | 2021 |
|---|---|---|---|
| AVERAGE HOUSE INCOME | 68,136 | 76,878 | 82,108 |
| MEDIAN HOUSE INCOME | 55,721 | 59,550 | 63,313 |
| PER CAPITA | 26,765 | 30,195 | 32,236 |

### RACIAL DIVERSITY

| CULTURE | 2010 | 2016 | 2021 |
|---|---|---|---|
| ASIAN | 208 | 221 | 238 |
| BLACK | 3,454 | 3,548 | 3,705 |
| WHITE | 11,688 | 11,785 | 12,189 |
| HISPANIC | 799 | 800 | 828 |
| OTHERS | 220 | 241 | 266 |

# CHURCH QUESTIONNAIRE

**SEX:** ☐ Male  ☐ Female

**AGE:**
- ☐ 0-12
- ☐ 13-19
- ☐ 20-29
- ☐ 30-39
- ☐ 40-49
- ☐ 50-59
- ☐ 60-75
- ☐ 76+

**DISTANCE LIVE FROM CHURCH:**
- ☐ less than 1 mile
- ☐ 2-5 miles
- ☐ 6-10 miles
- ☐ 10+ miles

**HOW LONG ATTENDED CHURCH:**
- ☐ less than 1 year
- ☐ 2-5 years
- ☐ 6-10 years
- ☐ 11-20 years
- ☐ 21+ years

**KIN WHO ATTEND OUTSIDE IMMEDIATE FAMILY:**
- ☐ 1-5 people
- ☐ 6-10 people
- ☐ 11-20 people
- ☐ 21+ people

**RATE THE FOLLOWING:**
1 – EXCELLENT   2 – GOOD
3 – OK          4 – WEAK
5 – NEEDS IMPROVING

\_\_\_\_\_ PREACHING
\_\_\_\_\_ WORSHIP SERVICE
\_\_\_\_\_ ADULT CHOIR
\_\_\_\_\_ PRAISE TEAM
\_\_\_\_\_ DEACONS
\_\_\_\_\_ NURSERY
\_\_\_\_\_ CHILDREN'S MINISTRY
\_\_\_\_\_ YOUTH MINISTRY
\_\_\_\_\_ SUNDAY SCHOOL
\_\_\_\_\_ FRIENDLINESS
\_\_\_\_\_ OUTREACH
\_\_\_\_\_ CHURCH APPEARANCE OUTSIDE CHURCH
\_\_\_\_\_ APPEARANCE INSIDE

**HOW OFTEN DO YOU ATTEND AM WORSHIP PER MONTH?**
☐ 1  ☐ 2  ☐ 3  ☐ 4

**HOW OFTEN DO YOU ATTEND PM WORSHIP PER MONTH?**
☐ 1  ☐ 2  ☐ 3  ☐ 4

EXAMPLE: For an average attendance of 100 on Sunday morning, a church will need 175 different people to attend during the month because everyone will not attend every Sunday.

**ANSWER THESE QUESTIONS:**
1. What area the strengths of our church?
2. What are the weaknesses of our church?
3. What is our church known for in the community?
4. What would you like to see your church do in the next five years?
5. What would you like to see your church do in the next ten years?

**INTERVIEW QUESTIONS:**
1. What are our greatest strengths?
2. What are our greatest weaknesses?
3. What would you like to see in five years?
4. What would you like to see in ten years?
5. What are our greatest problems?

# STATISTICAL CHARTS

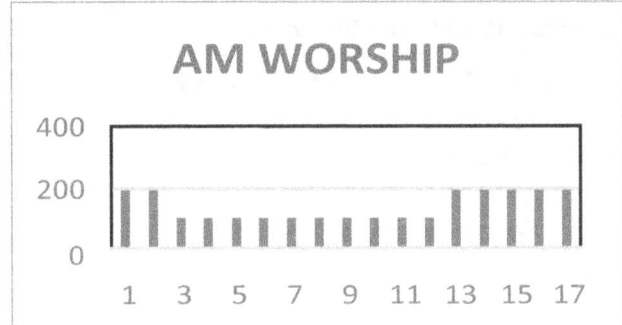
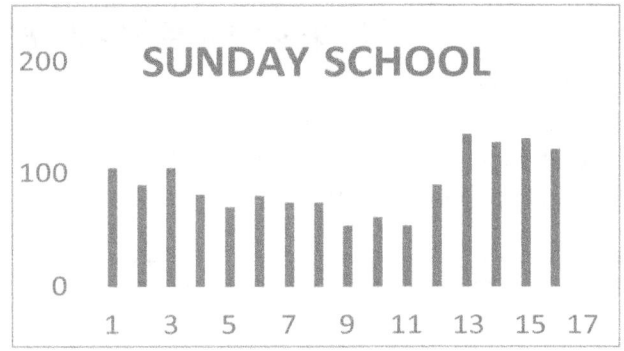
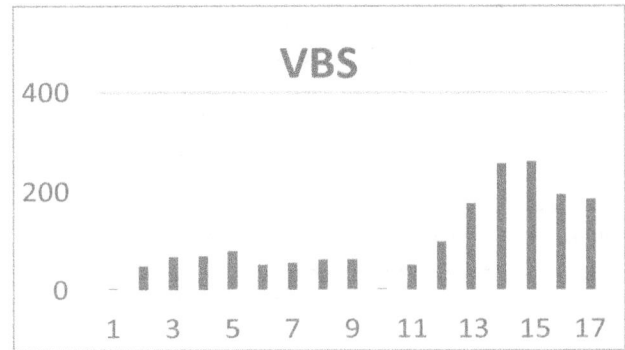
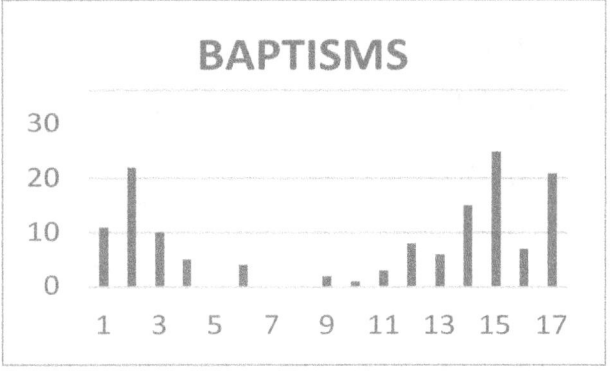
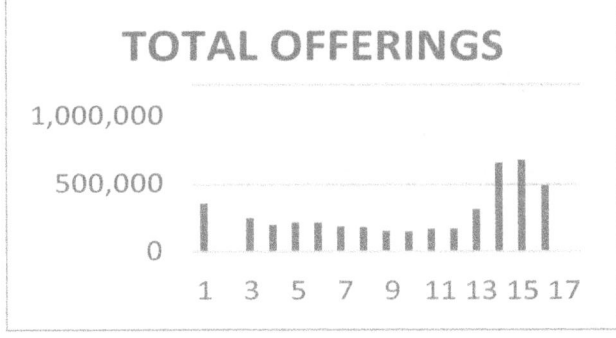
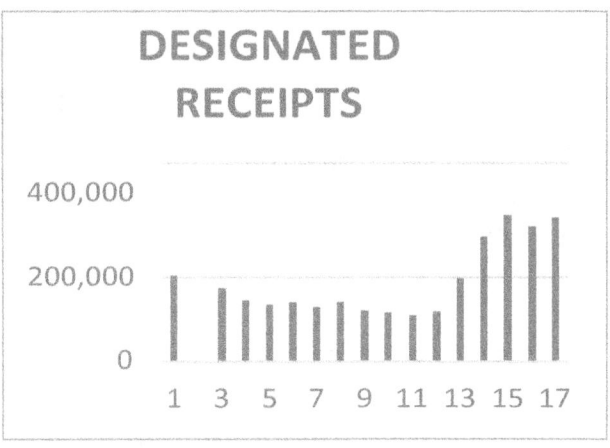
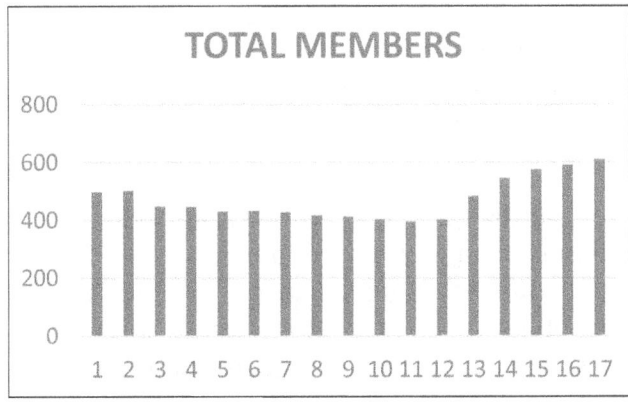

# GROWTH PROFILE SUMMARY

## OUR STRENGTHS (FROM QUESTIONNAIRE AND INTERVIEWS)

| STRENGTHS: | WHAT ARE OUR GREATEST STRENGTHS? |
|---|---|
| Worship service Preaching<br>Adult choir Deacon leadership<br>Caring for one another | Vacation Bible Schools We are a sleeping giant<br>Strong heritage<br>Quick response to people in need<br>Sunday School teachers |

**SSBC** has an aging membership with a few strong young families. They have a strong desire to see the church grow and do not want the church to die. They realize that relocation is a must.

## GROWTH TRENDS (2000-2012)

| DECLINE: | PLATEAU: | GROWTH: |
|---|---|---|
| Sunday School<br>Total Membership<br>Mission Gifts | | Tithes and Offerings<br>Cooperative Program |

The church is in a state of plateau and decline. Tithes and offerings have grown steadily, but behind inflation. Sunday school attendance has declined drastically during the past ten years. Offerings will not support full-time pastor.

**COMMENTS:** There is a sufficient population base within five miles of the church to sustain an average attendance of 200-250, providing an effective outreach program were implemented.

## MEMBERSHIP TRENDS

| | |
|---|---|
| 25% attend every Sunday<br>0% attend 2 or 3 Sundays<br>25% attend 1 Sunday | 64% live within 5 miles of church<br>36% live beyond 5 miles |

**COMMENTS:**

## OUR WEAKNESSES (FROM QUESTIONNAIRE AND INTERVIEWS)

| | |
|---|---|
| Pastoral leadership weak past 10 yrs<br>In stage 5 of 6 stages before death<br>Terminal diseases—location, average age 60+ | No ongoing projects<br>A few doing all the work<br>One person having too many jobs |

**COMMENTS:**
Many of the above comments result when a church is dissatisfied with the pastoral leadership. During the past few months, I believe **SSBC** has turned the corner and is headed back upward in spirit and desire to serve the Lord. There has been a rise in offerings and attendance. **THE LITTLE CHURCH WITH THE BIG HEART IS ON THE MOVE.** Members are getting more eager to serve the Lord. Finding a good pastor is the key to making right many of the above weaknesses. Remember, a pastor cannot do it by himself.

| WHAT WOULD YOU LIKE TO SEE SSBC DO IN THE NEXT FIVE YEARS? ||
|---|---|
| See attendance increase<br>Develop organized outreach<br>Call a dynamic preacher of the Word<br>**BUILD AND RELOCATE**<br>Regular fellowships<br>Continue children's sermon in worship service | Set both long-range and short-range goals<br>Get a good staff to lead us |
| **COMMENTS:** ||
| **SSBC** must not wait until securing a pastor to set short- and long-term goals. It will be so helpful to share with the prospective pastor your dreams and visions. All of the above suggestions are doable providing we prioritize and get to work. Remember, you cannot do everything at once. With God all things are possible! ||

BY COMPLETING THIS PROFILE SUMMARY YOU WILL GET AN ACCURATE SYNOPSIS OF YOUR CHURCH. THIS SHOULD HELP WITH YOUR PLANNING.

## TWELVE RECOMMENDATIONS PRESENTED BY DR. FOWLER

| RECOMMENDATIONS | EXPLANATIONS |
|---|---|
| **RECOMMENDATION #1:**<br>**ADMINISTRATIVE**<br>1. DEVELOP JOB DESCRIPTIONS: policies, vacations, etc.<br>2. DEVELOP new logo, newsletter format, all printed matter; maintain webpage.<br>3. MAINTAIN databases—mailing lists, prospects.<br>4. DEVELOP and maintain Facebook page.<br><br>**REASON:** to provide more modern look, and keep up with members and prospects. | **EXPLANATION #1**<br>These deal with the **ADMINISTRATION** of the church. In expectation of growth, an associate pastor will be needed. Responsibilities will include youth and children's ministry and preaching responsibilities on Sunday night. The AP will assist the pastor in visitation of the hospitalized and sick at home as needed.<br>**LOGO DEVELOPMENT:** It is important to develop a new image. The logo will be used on letterheads, newsletters, bulletins, and all other printed matter.<br>**FACEBOOK** presence in this day is vital.<br><br>**DATABASES** are a tool to manage prospects, mailing lists, etc. |
| **RECOMMENDATION #2:**<br>**SUNDAY SCHOOL**<br>1. Combine adult IV, V, VI into two classes.<br>2. Begin class for married adults 25-40.<br>3. Strengthen new class for single young adults.<br>4. **DEVELOP OUTREACH** visitation through SS.<br><br>**REASON:** space and need to prepare for growth. | **EXPLANATION #2**<br>**SUNDAY SCHOOL:** Looking at current classes and the number of people, we need to combine three adult classes into two. Need to begin a new class for married adults 25-40.<br>**NEED TO ADD:** A single young adult class with college students and working adults.<br>**OUTREACH:** Important to visit, call, or write all absentees. Church visitors need a home visit. |

| RECOMMENDATIONS (continued) | EXPLANATIONS (continued) |
|---|---|
| **RECOMMENDATION #3:**<br>**YOUTH HOUSE**<br>The church acquired a modular building with two restrooms, two large rooms, and an office. **THIS BUILDING WILL BE USED AS A YOUTH HOUSE.** Sunday School, Wednesday night Bible study, fellowships, games. | **EXPLANATION #3**<br>**YOUTH HOUSE:** Youth will paint, decorate, and furnish it under the adult leader's supervision. There is not a room in the main church that would provide this space. |
| **RECOMMENDATION #4:**<br>**ERECT ELECTRONIC SIGN**<br>On NC 97 in front of church, advertise events, special days, announcements, ETC.<br>**REASON:** 6000-7000 cars pass daily on NC 97; good, cost-effective advertising. | **EXPLANATION #4**<br>The electronic sign **WILL BE** a valuable advertising tool. This was a hard sell to the church. The one we purchased was approximately $15,000. |
| **RECOMMENDATION #5:**<br>**SUNDAY NIGHT SERVICE**<br>Change the structure for Sunday night to include a variety of services, including film night, a musical service, and group fellowship in homes. | **EXPLANATION #5**<br>Sunday night attendance had been declining for years and was down to 35-40. Realized there was a good number, primarily older people, who wanted to keep the night service. So I recommended that we have a variety of services—guest musical groups, a film about every two months, and special speakers. This has proven to be very successful. |
| **RECOMMENDATION #6:**<br>**SECRETARY SKILLS**<br>**SECRETARY:** Needs computer skills; to be efficient in XL, PowerPoint, and Word; to be able to operate office equipment; to have people skills; to have receptionist skills.<br><br>**RECOMMENDATION #7:**<br>**MINISTER OF YOUTH/CHILDREN**<br>Will direct ministries for these ages.<br><br>**RECOMMENDATION #8:**<br>**MINISTER OF MUSIC/WORSHIP LEADER**<br>Will direct adult choir; develop praise team and children's choir.<br>**REASON:** to provide quality ministries. | **EXPLANATION #6,7,8:**<br>**STAFFING CONCERNS**<br>These recommendations deal with staffing. We will need a **SECRETARY** who is computer literate and is able to use the Microsoft Office software package.<br><br>**MINISTER OF YOUTH/CHILDREN** will be an associate pastor who can deal with whatever comes up from preaching to assisting in funerals to training workers.<br><br>**WORSHIP LEADER** should be able to lead the music, develop an age-graded music program, and develop a praise team. |

| RECOMMENDATIONS (continued) | EXPLANATIONS (continued) |
|---|---|
| **RECOMMENDATION #9:**<br>**DEVELOP EFFECTIVE OUTREACH PROGRAM**<br>1. Identify unchurched people within five miles.<br>2. Mail regularly to residents who have indicated interest.<br>3. Make personal visit to all visitors<br>4. Maintain prospect database.<br>5. Have outreach event once every quarter.<br><br>**REASON:** get to know the community needs and meet them. | **RECOMMENDATION #9:**<br>**OUTREACH TEAM**<br>**AN OUTREACH TEAM** is a must to follow up with all the visitors who come to Southside. The Fall Festival attracts 500-900 registered visitors. VBS and Upward Soccer attract another several hundred.<br><br>**Matthew 9:37-38 (KJV)**<br>*Then saith he unto his disciples, The harvest truly is plenteous, but the labourers are few; Pray ye therefore the Lord of the harvest, that he will send forth labourers into his harvest.* |
| **RECOMMENDATION #10:**<br>Make a greater effort to reach our Upward Soccer and our softball families. | **RECOMMENDATION #10:**<br>**OUTREACH TEAM**<br>**AN OUTREACH TEAM** is a must to follow up with all the visitors who come to Southside. The Fall Festival attracts 500-900 registered visitors. VBS and Upward Soccer attract another several hundred.<br><br>**Matthew 9:37-38 (KJV)**<br>*Then saith he unto his disciples, The harvest truly is plenteous, but the labourers are few; Pray ye therefore the Lord of the harvest, that he will send forth labourers into his harvest.* |
| **RECOMMENDATION #11:**<br>**PHASE II BUILDING**<br>1. **BUILD A FAMILY LIFE CENTER**<br>Include classrooms and stage when our current building is sold. Give room for plays, concerts.<br>2. **BUILD SOFTBALL FIELDS**<br><br>After school for kids' basketball teams, indoor volleyball, walking tracks. | **RECOMMENDATION #11:**<br>**PHASE II BUILDING**<br>The recommendation is self-explanatory. This type of building will allow Southside to increase the ministries that could be offered to the community. |
| **RECOMMENDATION #12:**<br>**CONSIDER CHURCH NAME**<br>Southside will become a regional church drawing people from Wilson, Nashville, Rocky Mount, Bailey, and eastern Wake County.<br><br>Southside will no longer be a neighborhood church. **SHOULD WE CHANGE THE NAME?** | **RECOMMENDATION #12:**<br>**NAME CHANGE**<br>After many made comments to me, I realized the importance of the name **SOUTHSIDE**. I withdrew this recommendation and it was never voted upon. |

# STEP #4: GETTING READY, 2009-2012

## TIMELINE

| Nov 15, 2009 | My first Sunday |
| --- | --- |
| Dec 30, 2009 | Began as interim |
| June 23, 2010 | Began as pastor |
| April 3, 2011 | Groundbreaking |
| June 2, 2011 | Tree of Life commitment |
| July 2011 | Began construction |
| Aug 21, 2011 | Last homecoming Church St |
| March 4, 2012 | First service on NC 97 |

## MY FIRST SUNDAY—NOVEMBER 15, 2009

I believe GOD saw a man that HE could use: with 50+ years of experience, I served eight interims; pastored four churches; served as associate pastor in one church; recruited 60,000 to go to home mission fields across the US; preached in 100+ churches; had been in every state in the US; had been in six foreign countries; and had a wonderful wife. With my Social Security and income sources, I was in a position that I did not need a full-time salary because Southside could not afford it. Money was not the issue early on, nor has it ever been. GOD picked me to lead this congregation from 2616 S. CHURCH STREET TO HWY 97. I had never led a church through a building program. The people loved on me and Beth and we loved them back. Wow, we were in for the experience of our lives.

## MY INITIAL WEEKS AND MONTHS

After each Sunday, Jim Joyner, chairman of deacons, asked me to come back again. I told Jim I would preach through December and then we would talk about the interim. During December, I began to SENSE that Southside was the place GOD WAS CALLING ME to serve. I felt that with my talents and experiences, this would be a GOOD FIT. I shared with the deacons that I wanted to meet with them to discuss the possibilities. Toward the end of December 2009, I met with the deacons.

## DISCUSSIONS WITH THE DEACONS: WHAT WOULD THEY EXPECT OF ME?

- Preach on Sunday mornings and Nights.
- Lead prayer meetings on Wednesday nights.
- Visit anyone who may be in the hospital or sick at home.

## I DISCUSSED THESE ISSUES WITH THE DEACONS:

- I shared my testimony.
- I shared my experience with church growth.
- I asked what were the immediate needs of Southside.
- I asked what they saw in the future.
- I asked what potential they saw.
- I asked what they wanted to do.
- I asked if they really wanted to relocate.
- I told them I would do a church growth study.
- I told them I would present the findings to the church.
- I told them I wanted the church to discuss and act on my recommendations.
- I told them I would do whatever I could to help the church.
- **I PROMISED TO QUIT IF THEY STARTED FUSSING** (they never fussed while I was there).

Questions I Thought About:
1. Is this where God is calling me to serve?
2. Am I really prepared for the challenge?

## RESULTS OF MEETING WITH THE DEACONS:

- They shared their expectations and concerns about their church with me.
- They answered the above questions.
- I shared my expectations and concerns with them.

- I shared my consulting experiences.
- TOGETHER we would figure out what to do.
- They asked me to be their interim pastor.
- I said I WOULD BE HAPPY TO SERVE AS SOUTHSIDE'S INTERIM PASTOR.
- We agreed on the compensation.
- After serving six weeks as the supply pastor, the first Sunday in January 2010, I officially became the interim pastor.

## SUMMARY OF MY BACKGROUND

CHECK: Some thought SOUTHSIDE WAS a hopeless and helpless challenge. The church's future was very FRAGILE. I LOVED A CHALLENGE SO HERE WE GO.

I talked with a long-time member. She shared that she had seriously thought about going to another church. Her husband said God had not led him to leave. They were hoping for a great TURNAROUND!!

## MY FIRST FEW MONTHS SERVING AS INTERIM PASTOR:

- I began making home visits
- I saw a group of people who did not want to quit, although quitting would have been the easiest decision.
- I worked pretty much full time and the church started to grow.

## I FELT THE LORD LEADING ME TO COME AND HELP THEM.

I would come under these conditions:
1. ALLOW me to do a CHURCH GROWTH STUDY. And I would present the results to the church. This process would take several months.
2. IF THEY STARTED FUSSING I would leave immediately.
3. TIME REQUIREMENTS: The deacons asked that I preach twice on Sundays, lead prayer meetings on Wednesdays, and visit the sick. I never saw working with SOUTHSIDE as a part-time ministry. In addition to the above expectations, I started visiting in the homes of the people. I have always felt that a pastor needs to get to know his flock. This can only be done through home visitation.

## WEDNESDAY NIGHT STUDIES

I began to teach about several issues we were facing.
1. DO YOU REALLY WANT TO RELOCATE on the property you purchased? In 1999 the church bought 21.4 acres of land on HWY 97 west of Rocky Mount, just pass the airport. The land was completely paid in full in just a few years.
2. THINGS WE WOULD FACE:
   - Assimilating new members
   - Changing ministry style
   - Changing staff
   - Accepting new members in leadership

## JANUARY 1, 2010 — I BEGAN SERVING AS INTERIM PASTOR

THE CURRENT BUILDING was beautiful and in wonderful condition. Building another building like this would cost two million.

- Sanctuary seated 350+/-.
- Good sound system was in place.
- Projection system for hymns and media.
- Red carpet was clean and traditional.
- The floors in the educational building were beautiful hardwoods and well kept.
- About ten people sang in a very traditional choir.
- The choir leader had served about eight years—his age was early to mid-seventies.
- The secretary was in her mid-sixties and had volunteered for many years.
- I was in my mid-sixties.
- We had a senior staff.

## DURING THESE EARLY MONTHS

I majored on several things:
- Preached positive, challenging messages.
- Led prayer meetings.

- Visited the sick, rest homes, and the homebound.
- Met regularly with the LRPC Long Range Planning Committee.
- Got to know the people by name by visiting them in their homes.
- Had several meetings with JOHN HAMM, Director of Missions of the NRBA.

## LONG RANGE PLANNING COMMITTEE

LRPC was composed of good solid and proven leaders. Four members were in their 40s, one was in their 70s, and one was in their 60s. All had been members a long time. Several had grown up in the church. Jerry Reams served as chairman. Debbie Parker, Pam Jackson, Grace Wallace, Cecil Reams, and Terry Tyson served on the LRPC.

## AN ASSESMENT FROM DEBBIE PARKER, WHO HAD BEEN A MEMBER ALL HER LIFE AND NOW WAS IN HER 40s

Serving on the Long Range Planning Committee during a time of transition and "unknowns" was both frustrating and exciting at the same time. The church body was down to its smallest membership/attendance since its charter. The congregation was predominantly older and fearful of the church closing. The entire Long Range Planning Committee had finally reached a consensus that for the church to survive, we had to relocate. Some members in the congregation, however, were determined to "stay put" until the current building was sold and we had enough money to pay for a new building. DEBT FREE. The greatest struggle for the Long Range Planning Committee was not the building plan itself; it was getting the church body to stop dwelling on where we had been and where we were rather than focusing on God's direction.

Even though efforts had been made to postpone a vote to build, the committee was able to convince the congregation that all of our waiting and the many trials were simply a test of faith and it was time to prove our faithfulness. The many frustrations leading up to the vote to build was soon overshadowed by the excitement of presenting the building plan and having it pass unanimously.

## AN ASSESMENT FROM PAM JACKSON WHO HAD BEEN A MEMBER ALL HER LIFE AND WAS NOW IN HER 40s

I was honored to serve on the Long Range Planning Committee. Many people said we would never move to the property on HWY 97; however, God had a PLAN and a TIME. Previous Long Range Planning Committees set the plan in motion to relocate and for their hard work I am very grateful. It is my belief that God put the right people together at the perfect time to accomplish the task that our church assigned them. The committee, as it stood prior to the move to HWY 97, was comprised of a group of people possessing diverse talents and experiences. This diversity made the committee strong and ultimately successful. There was much thought and planning put into every step even when it meant going back to square one. Whenever there was an obstacle, we worked through it and never moved on without a unanimous decision. It was only after our church made the decision to take "A LEAP OF FAITH" that our dream to build a church started to become a reality. Serving on this committee was stressful at times, but more than that very rewarding.

## SUMMARY
## THE GOAL OF THE LRPC:
- **LEAD IN BUILDING A CHURCH**
- **MONITOR BUILDING PLANS**
- **EXPLORE FUNDING POSSIBILITIES**
- **RELOCATE:** Selling the old building was no longer the priority. A set of plans had been developed by an earlier committee with a building over two million.
- **MUST DEPEND UPON GOD TO SELL THE BUILDING**

## WE TALKED ABOUT WHAT TYPE OF BUILDING WE WANTED AND HOW MUCH IT WOULD COST. These things were suggested:

- Family life center—multi-use space
- Kitchen
- Bathrooms
- Staff offices
- Classrooms
- Worship space
- Adequate parking
- Sanctuary

## Exploring the Finances

### LOCAL BANKS

I approached two local banks. After we discussed our tithes and offerings, they both told us that current offerings were not large enough to make the building payment and weekly expenses. Neither bank considered loaning money to us.

### THE NC BAPTIST FOUNDATION

Their purpose is to make church construction loans primarily to Baptist churches. They are a part of the Baptist State Convention of NC. Russell Jones is the representative in Eastern NC.

> How much building we could build would be determined by available funds plus the amount we could borrow.

### AFTER SEVERAL CONVERSATIONS, MR. JONES OF THE NC BAPTIST FOUNDATION WANTED THIS INFORMATION:

- Past three year finances
- List of outstanding debts
- Current treasurer's report
- Current budget
- List of current assets and property values
- The amount we wanted to borrow
- Copy of the building plans

We gathered this information and submitted it to him. He made no promises but said he would see what the foundation could do.

### OUR ASSETS:

- Our existing building—tax value 1.25 million, debt free
- 21.5 acres of land, debt free—$250,000
- Building fund had grown to $350,000

### BAPTIST FOUNDATION OFFER

After reviewing our finances, the NCBF determined they could loan us $600,000. Adding this to the $400,000 in the building fund since the land was paid in full, we could build a $1,000,000 project including furnishings, structure, parking lot, etc. Current interest rates were 6.25 percent.

THE LRPC team decided we wanted SMITHSON, a local turnkey contractor, to build our building. There were several meetings with Daniel Proctor of Smithson and his team. They started drawing the plans we wanted. WE APPROVED EACH STEP.

> Please note: We recommend the NCBF to any church wanting to build.

After paying on the loan for a couple years, the interest rate was reduced to 4.9 percent. Later, after establishing a payment history, we refinanced with a local bank that reduced our interest to 3.5 percent. This refinance saved us approximately $10,000 per year.

### THE DONOR TREE

We asked the church to pray about making a three-year commitment to give extra to the building fund to make payments on the new building.

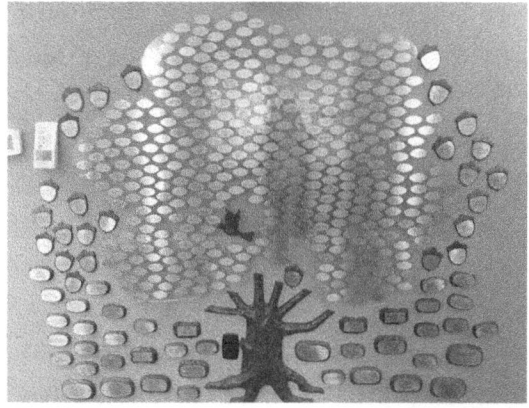

## WE USED A DONOR TREE

According to size of the donation, you could get a leaf, small stone, large stone, or an engraved acorn to place on the tree. This could be in honor or in memory of someone.

## Leap of Faith Campaign

### 1. WE DEVELOPED A THEME.

### 2. WE DEVELOPED A COMMITMENT CARD.

### 3. WE SET THE COMMITMENT DAY AND GOAL.

We asked everyone to turn in their commitment card by a certain date.

**GOAL:** $3,500 PER MONTH
We promoted the date and the amount NEEDED several weeks in the bulletin and newsletter.

**RESULTS:** We had commitments for more than enough to make the building payments.

### 4. ACTION REQUIRED: A LEAP OF FAITH.

## DONOR TREE FOR BUILDING FUND

**LEAF**
Donation of $500—$999
Up to 3 lines imprint

**SMALL STONE**
Donation of $1000—$1900
Up to 6 lines imprint

**LARGE STONE**
Donation of $2000—$2499
Up to 6 lines imprint

**ACORN**
Donation of $2500 or more
UP to 6 lines imprint

### THE LEAP OF FAITH CAMPAIGN

In the fall of 2010, the pastor was preaching and gave a challenge: "Do you really want to build?" EVERYONE STOOD. Noticing a consensus, he said, "I am going to set the date for the groundbreaking: **APRIL 3, 2011**."

# STEP #5: MOVING FORWARD

## BUILDING THE INITIAL BUILDING

It was so exciting. Personally, I have never been in a church with a building project underway. Everything was new to me as well as to most of our people. It took us several steps to get to this point.

1. Church made decision to build.
2. LRPC worked with local turnkey contractor to design the building.
3. LEAP OF FAITH CAMPAIGN WAS SUCCESSFUL. Church committed to give $3,500 per month for building payments for three years.
4. LEAP OF FAITH CAMPAIGN helped us to determine how much we could build.
5. Arranged financing with NCBF—The North Carolina Baptist Foundation.
6. OUR RESOURCES: Land was debt free and we had $300,000 in the building fund. NCBF would loan us $700,000.
7. FUNDS AVAILABLE: $1,000,000.
8. JERRY REAMS served as HVAC contractor.

*I was designated as honorary building contractor. I went out every day to see what was happening and to offer my opinion.*

Septic tank looked like a swimming pool

# Our First Sunday: 305 Attended

A view from the front of the church. A cross was inlaid with brick at both the front and rear apex

An attractive, computer-controlled led sign was installed by the highway near the front entrance. It attracts many visitors. Our first Sunday below.

## Preparing for the First Sunday

**GETTING THE BUILDING READY**

Everyone worked so hard getting the building ready.
- BOUGHT new tables
- BOUGHT 450 chairs
- ERECTED cross on back wall
- ATTACHED DONOR TREE on front wall near entrance
- BOUGHT FURNITURE for front lobby
- INSTALLED telephone and alarm systems
- MOVED office equipment from Church Street
- SMITHSON, INC. paved the parking lot, cemented the sidewalks, finished the building
- INSTALLED big screen TVs and sound equipment in worship center
- OVERFLOW ROOM—set up one room with monitor just in case
- CHURCH YARD looked superb
- YOUTH BUILDING was perfect
- RESTROOMS were well stocked
- NEW PULPIT was in place
- PIANO was on stage
- ***PASTOR WAS NERVOUS.***
- SOUTHSIDE had bought land 12 years earlier.
- DREAM WAS ABOUT TO COME TRUE.
- SOME WHO HAD THE DREAM HAD DIED.

**MY THOUGHTS:**
- How many would actually show up?
- Would we have enough seats?
- Would there be enough parking?
- Would my sermon be good?
- Would people return?

**I WAS REMINDED OF A SCRIPTURE:**

*Psalm 55:22 (KJV)*
*Cast thy burden upon the LORD, and he shall sustain thee: he shall never suffer the righteous to be moved.*

**SCRIPTURE TEACHES:**
- Cast your burdens and cares on the Lord
- No need to worry
- God has control of this

This helped relieve my nerves some.

**I THOUGHT BACK TO 1989.**
- I was asked to be a church planter in Greenville.
- The Baptist Association wanted to start a new church in the hospital area.
- Three sponsoring churches wanted to be a part of the new work.
- We secured the Holiday Inn's meeting room.
- Volunteers made 7000 phone calls.
- They asked if people were involved in a church.
- If not, they asked if they could mail some information to them about a new church.
- 700 families requested our information.
- NIGHT BEFORE JITTERS SET IN.
- How many would show up?
- Would we have enough space?
- ***One hundred sixty*** showed up the first Sunday.
- ***Ten*** of these were pastor's children and had not been in a church in ten years.

### GOD IS IN CONTROL!!

## The First Sunday and Beyond

**FIRST SUNDAY FINALLY ARRIVED
MARCH 4, 2012**

# WOW!!!

# 305

**WHOEVER WOULD HAVE THOUGHT!! TO GOD BE THE GLORY!!!**

## PROBLEM FROM DAY ONE: BUILDING WAS TOO SMALL

Attendance on Church Street before we moved was 75-100.

1. We built all we could afford to build.
2. NO ONE, including me, ever had an idea that attendance would be 305 the first Sunday.
3. OUR ATTENDANCE JUMPED BY THREE TIMES IN ONE SUNDAY.
4. SPACE ISSUES: The worship space could comfortably handle 210 or two-thirds of the attendance. Church growth specialists tell us that when attendance exceeds 80 percent of your seating capacity, growth is limited.
5. We had people sitting in two overflow rooms watching the service on a monitor.
6. PARKING ISSUES: NOT ENOUGH SPACES. Cars were parked on the side of the highway and also in the parking lot and at the convenience store across the street. Cars were parked funeral home style—in rows.

I WAS THE ONLY MINISTER. How does one person follow up all these PEOPLE?

---

Our needs were apparent
- Not enough seating
- Not enough parking
- Not enough staff

What a problem to have!

---

## POSSIBLE SOLUTIONS

1. DO TWO AM SERVICES. I did not act on this for of three reasons.
   - I did not want to divide the church.
   - Two AM services plus the night service would require lot of energy.
   - We did not have musicians in place to handle two AM services.
2. TRY TO FIND A STAFF PERSON WHO COULD HELP ME.
   - I knew a couple waiting to go to the mission field who lived in Rocky Mount. I had known the man for several years.

## I BELIEVED GOD WOULD PROVIDE

### Problems to Resolve

**SEVERAL ISSUES TO RESOLVE**
- INSUFFICIENT PARKING
- INSUFFICIENT SEATING
- INSUFFICIENT STAFF
- INSUFFICIENT LEADERS
- VISITOR FOLLOW-UP
- PREPARING FOR NEW MEMBERS

## WHAT DO YOU DO? PRAY, PRAY, PRAY

### INSUFFICIENT PARKING

We paved enough parking for 175 vehicles. We needed to enlarge our parking. I asked Jerry Reams how much it would cost to expand the parking lot. He got an estimate of $25,000. We had built to the max. Where would we get another $25,000?

I prayed, "Lord you know where this money will come from. I DON'T." And it was amazing to see how God supplies. That very afternoon a member came by the church and said she had a check to give to the church. Her mother had died and left some money in her will for the church. The check was for exactly $25,000. We talked about where to use it. I told the lady about the parking lot need. She agreed to put it there. IN JUST A FEW WEEKS, OUR PARKING LOT WAS EXPANDED.

### INSUFFICIENT SEATING

WE HAD TWO CHOICES:
1. Two AM services
2. Enlarge building

After discussing the best way to handle it, we decided to take out the back wall. This would give us space for
- three Sunday School classes,

- a storage room,
- a choir room,
- and a stage.

Estimates were in the $350,000 - $400,000 range for a building addition. It took about a year, until March 2013, to break ground.

Construction was completed by the end of the year. During this time, one member came in and handed me a check for $45,000. This gift helped tremendously. Others continued TO GIVE AND GIVE.

## INSUFFICIENT STAFF

Our deacons and others were doing what they could. But I needed staff help. Our budget was uncertain. Our old budget could hardly pay my salary. What were we going to do? Who would we find?

Again, GOD WAS TESTING OUR FAITH.

I PRAYED AND PRAYED. JACK GIVENS kept coming to mind. Jack had been associate pastor of Englewood Baptist Church. I had known Jack, as my wife and I were members at Englewood for 12 years prior to coming to Southside. He and his wife were waiting to go to India as international missionaries with the SBC International Mission Board. I called Jack and asked him to have lunch with me.

I told Jack we could pay him $400 per week. That was much lower than he was accustomed to. He had about four months he could help us. My wife and I prayed about it and we both agreed that we would pay him $400 per week and take it from my $700 per week salary. *HE AGREED TO HELP US.*

## IT IS MORE BLESSED TO GIVE THAN TO RECEIVE. GOD BLESSED US FOR DOING THAT.

### JACK'S MINISTRY FOCUS

1. Jack taught a class for people interested in knowing more about Southside, for potential new members.
2. Jack taught a senior adult Bible study on Tuesday mornings with an average of 50 people attending.
3. Jack prayed with me and encouraged me in FINDING THE ANSWER TO "WHAT DO I DO NEXT?"
4. Jack preached on Sunday nights.

JACK WAS A TREMENDOUS HELP and a real encouragement to me. He began with us around the end of MARCH and would be leaving in JUNE. So we had to figure out the next step.

ATTENDANCE was remaining steady
225-235 on Sunday AM
100-125 on Sunday PM

## JACK WOULD LEAVE IN JUNE. WHAT THEN?

AS JUNE WAS FAST APPROACHING, I asked during Wednesday night prayer meetings, "Does anyone know someone who would make us a good associate pastor?" Billy Vick said, "I sure do. CJ CAUBLE."

CJ CAUBLE was a former youth minister at Union Missionary Baptist Church. He moved upon graduation from Southeastern Baptist Seminary. Billy gave me his telephone number. I called and asked for a resume and discussed his interest in coming to help us.

CJ CAUBLE became our Associate Pastor with

Youth and Children and had the responsibility of preaching on Sunday nights. He and his family moved to Southside in June 2012.

## WHAT I LEARNED FROM THE 305 PEOPLE

We HAD to identify people to take leadership roles immediately.
- We could not wait for an individual to be a member for a year.
- We had to determine how to follow up with all these people.
- Visit with as many people as possible to learn their names, where they lived, and how to minister to them
- Identify leadership skills

---

I called the NC Baptist convention for help. My question: What do you do when your church grows from 100 to 305 in one week?

---

## THEIR RESPONSES:
- That is a good question.
- I never heard of this happening.
- I will pray that you figure it out.
- Harry, if anyone can figure it out, you can.

## EXAMINING THE 305
1. About 25 were my wife's relatives.
2. About 100-125 were original Southside members.
3. About 100 were from a neighboring church looking for a NEW place to worship.
4. About 75-100 people lived in the community and were not involved in a church.
5. About 25-35 rode by the church and saw it being built and curiosity led them to the first service.
6. A high percentage of people completed an information card. We began building a database.
7. We used nametags hoping many would wear them.

MY DIRECTOR OF MISSIONS, REV. JOHN HAMM, was more help than anyone.
- He always was willing to listen.
- He offered some insights to think about.
- JOHN HAS BECOME A DEAR FRIEND. I APPRECIATE HIM VERY MUCH. HE ALWAYS HAS TIME FOR YOU WHEN YOU CALL.

---

THAT IS WHY I AM WRITING THIS BOOK. TO SHARE WHAT I LEARNED ALONG THIS JOURNEY. MY PRAYER IS THIS BOOK WILL BE A BLESSING TO YOUR MINISTRY.

---

## THE THREE GROUPS ON FIRST SUNDAY
GROUP #1: 100 FROM ONE CHURCH
1. These people were very sensitive and did not want to upset the balance or ways we did ministry.
2. This group was meeting in an apartment complex meeting room. A deacon and I went tox meet with them. I assured them they would be welcomed. We invited them to be part of our church. I told them that we needed their help to develop our church ministries.
3. We had been praying to the Lord of the Harvest to send us laborers. I told them, "YOU ARE AN ANSWER TO OUR PRAYERS."
4. I OPENED THE DOOR WIDE FOR THEM TO COME AND THEY DID.

**P.S. THESE PEOPLE HAVE BEEN SUCH A HUGE BLESSING TO SOUTHSIDE.**

GROUP #2: 75-100 FROM THE COMMUNITY
1. We mailed visitors letters telling them how glad we were to have them on our first Sunday. We encouraged them to come back.
2. I called as many as I could and talked with them. I found most of them had enjoyed their first service and were very receptive.
3. Southside folks helped by calling the rest of the visitors.

4. These people were from a ten-mile radius—Wilson, Bailey, Nashville, Rocky Mount, Spring Hope, Sharpsburg, and all points in between.
5. One thing that helped us was our high visibility on a well-traveled road where 7000 cars per day traveled.

GROUP #3: THE SOUTHSIDE FOLKS
- GOD had answered our prayer.
- They were so excited to see all the people.
- GOD had sent us laborers to work in the harvest field.
- We have completed the move from Church Street to HWY 97.
- A 12-year dream HAD COME TRUE.

**AFTER A FEW WEEKS,**
- PEOPLE STARTED JOINING THE CHURCH.
- TITHES AND OFFERINGS INCREASED.
- PEOPLE WERE WILLING TO WORK AND WERE ASKING US, "WHAT CAN I DO?"
- THE CHOIR DOUBLED.
- WORSHIP ATTENDANCE TRIPLED.
- THERE WERE BAPTISMS, NEW MEMBERS, AND SMILES. Since we had no baptistry, we used member's swimming pools.
- MISSION GIFTS TRIPLED.

## BUILDING ENLARGEMENT BECAME A TOP PRIORITY

On our first anniversary, we broke ground for expansion. After checking with several contractors, we chose Mr. Maye of Louisburg. The expansion would include four classrooms, one storage room, additional parking, and additional seating for 200. Cost of this expansion would be approximately $500,000.

People would not keep coming if there were no place to sit.

**To the left of the black line is the original building. To the right is the additional building.**

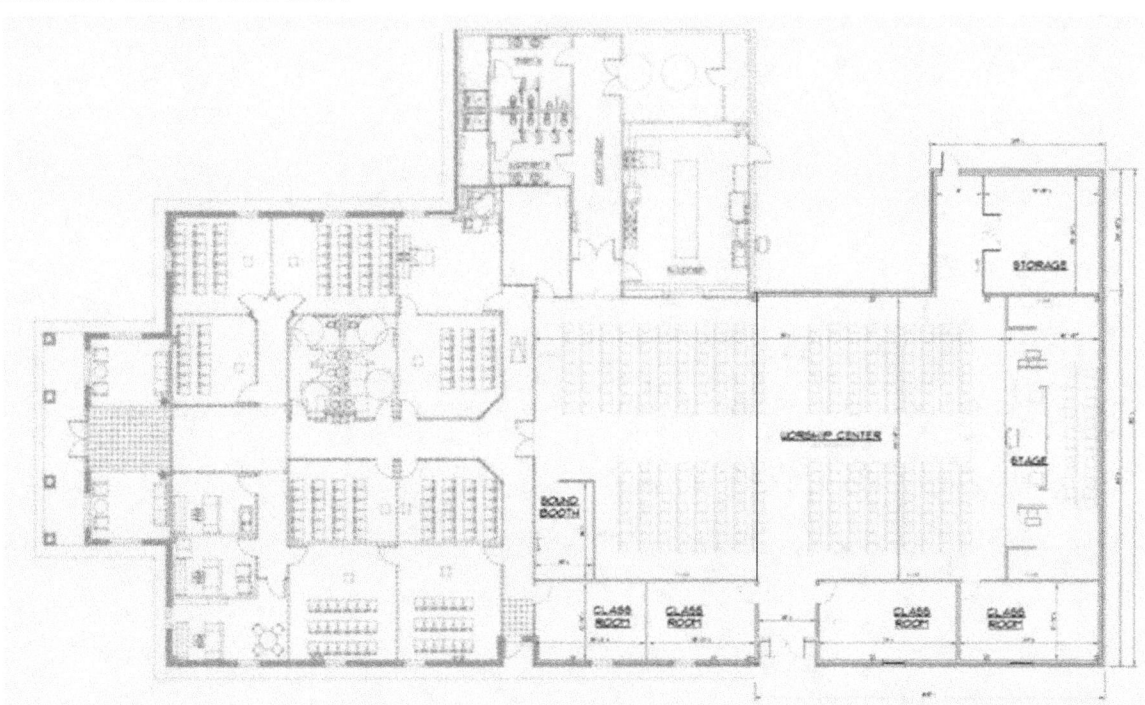

# STEP #6: WHAT NEXT?

## FIRST SUNDAY WAS A TREMENDOUS SUCCESS
1. MUCH PLANNING AND PRAYER WENT INTO THAT FIRST SUNDAY.
2. THE BUILDING WAS PREPARED.
3. FIVE THOUSAND POSTCARDS WERE MAILED TO RESIDENTS WITHIN FIVE MILES OF THE CHURCH.
4. ATTENDANCE WAS BEYOND EXPECTATION.
5. PEOPLE CAME—ATTENDANCE JUMPED FROM 124 TO 305 IN ONE WEEK.
6. WORSHIP SPACE ONLY HELD 215. MANY IN OVERFLOW ROOM.
7. NOT ENOUGH PARKING SPACES.
8. NO PLANNED FOLLOW-UP WAS IN PLACE.
9. CHILDREN, YOUTH, AND YOUNG FAMILIES WERE EVERYWHERE.

## WHAT IS THE NEXT STEP?
- DISTINGUISH BETWEEN POTENTIAL MEMBERS AND VISITORS.
- SEND LETTERS TO ALL WHO GAVE US THEIR ADDRESS.
- SEND EMAILS TO ALL WHO GAVE US EMAIL ADDRESSES.
- IDENTIFY FOUR BASIC GROUPS:
    - ORIGINAL SOUTHSIDE    100
    - PEOPLE FROM UNION    100
    - NEIGHBORHOOD    80
    - FOWLER RELATIVES    25

## WHAT WE DISCOVERED
- Some came to be part of the first Sunday.
- Some came looking for a church.
- Some had been watching the building going up and came out of curiosity.
- A sizable number completed information cards with name, address, email, and phone number.
- Some became regular attenders and later joined.
- Some never came back.

## FOLLOW-UP
- We were overwhelmed by the numbers.
- The deacons and others helped me call visitors to tell them we were so glad they had come and hoped they would come again.
- Jack Givens, former associate pastor at Englewood, and IMB missionary to India, came and helped me for three and a half months.
- Jack taught Bible study on Tuesday mornings to about 45, primarily senior adults.
- He also taught a potential new members class we called Discovering Southside.
- Seventy-nine people attended the four-week potential new member class. He taught this class during Sunday School.
- I made as many home visits as possible to get to know the people.

## WHAT PEOPLE WANTED TO KNOW
- The type of church we were going to be.
- The pastor's vision for the church.
- Were we visitor friendly?
- Did our church want newcomers?

## MY COMMENTS:
- Not every church is visitor friendly. Many churches have power issues and do not want to share their responsibilities with newcomers.
- The more family related a church is, the greater this problem. Southside was not a family church.
- The pastor sets the atmosphere in the service. One of the gifts God gave me was the gift of hospitality and the ability to make people feel at home.
- When we initially talked about relocating we knew we did not have ample leaders to staff the church if we grew significantly.

- We prayed to the Lord of the Harvest that he would send forth laborers. And send HE did.
- Some of the people who came were deacons, teachers, tithers, leaders, encouragers. I prayed that the Lord would let me identify people and their gifts.
- Normally a church likes to know their new members several months before they are given responsibilities.
- NOT TRUE WITH SOUTHSIDE. As soon as we identified people and their gifts we put them to work. We did keep the deacon requirement that they be members for at least one year.
- It was so challenging and so much fun getting to know everyone.
- I began teaching on Wednesday nights the vision of the church as I saw it.

**THE HARVEST TRULY WAS PLENTEOUS**
- One Sunday there were 19 who joined the church.
- Two Sundays there were 10.

**HOW DO YOU GET TO KNOW THIS MANY PEOPLE?**
- We had a Lay Renewal Weekend. This weekend had teaching in both large and small groups. This gave the opportunity to learn people on a first name basis.
- NAME TAGS: People wore nametags until they were sick of nametags.

## TEN STEP ASSIMILATION PROCESS

Assimilating new members is an important key to the growth and revitalization of a church. As you will notice in many churches, people join the church but attendance never increases. This is often referred to as the BACK DOOR PROBLEM. People are coming in the FRONT DOOR and others are leaving out the BACK DOOR.

1. YOUR CHURCH must become MY CHURCH. It takes a while for the new members to feel at home. It takes time for a new member to learn names.
2. NEW MEMBERS need to find a place to serve. The quicker the better. When Southside grew so rapidly, I taught a spiritual gifts course. This class was well attended and well received. We attempted to identify what people were gifted to do. One week our attendance was 125 and the next week it was 305. While all the visitors were not prospects, many were. I attempted to informally interview all new members to see where they had worked in the past and what interests they had in working in the future. I asked for testimonies during Sunday and Wednesday night services in an effort to quickly encourage everyone to get to know each other. To be eligible for the role of deacon, a person was required to be a member of the church for one year. There were no other time lengths required in order to serve.

**CHURCH GROWTH INSTITUTE has an excellent Spiritual Gifts course.**

3. NEW MEMBERS must make at least six new friends in six months or they become targets for leaving via the BACK DOOR. While the pastor's preaching and the teacher's teaching are important, fellowship and friendship are key for people to become a part of the church. Monthly church fellowships, Wednesday night suppers, occasional donuts and coffee on Sunday mornings are key events.
4. NEW MEMBERS need to be involved in Sunday morning Sunday School or small groups. Being a member of a group gives accountability. If someone is going to have surgery, no one would know if they were not involved in a group. Also, if a regular worship attender misses several weeks in a row, no one would miss them.

5. NEW MEMBERS need to understand the history of the church. Churches have unique personalities. Every church has strengths and weaknesses. It is important for new members to understand the past.
6. NEW MEMBERS need to understand the vision of the church. What is the church wanting to do in the next five to ten years? Southside grew so rapidly, it was almost like having a new church. New members needed to be included in the vision. On the first anniversary of our move, we broke ground to expand our seating from 200 to 400 and to add additional classrooms and a storage room. As the church looks toward the next phase of expansion, there are three thoughts. ONE, a family life center, which would include a gym. TWO, an educational building for additional Sunday School classes. THREE, a sanctuary. There are NOT enough funds to build all three. In the near future, the church will have to decide which direction to go. The pastor is the key vision caster. Occasionally, in sermons and on Wednesday nights, he needs to share the VISION for the future.
7. NEW MEMBERS need to know the ins and the outs of the organizational structure. How does the church make decisions? When is the annual budget done? How are the officers and teachers chosen and elected? How are deacons selected? How does the church call pastors and staff? The constitution and bylaws spell out these procedures. Sometimes a church will realize parts of the constitution and bylaws are outdated. What is the process for making changes?
8. NEW MEMBERS must know and understand what the church believes. What are the basic doctrines of the church? We follow a document known as the Baptist Faith and Message. We practice baptism by immersion. We believe in the eternal security of the believer. We believe salvation is by faith and not works. Anyone who is a Christian can take the Lord's Supper with us.
9. NEW MEMBERS must understand the expectations of church membership. If a person joins a church, they should attend regularly, give regularly, and participate in the ministry of the church. A church member should not be a gossiper or backbiter. A church member should do all they can to keep peace and unity in the church.
10. NEW MEMBERS would benefit from participating in a Lay Renewal Weekend. This event is held on the weekend. The weekend includes large and small groups both in the church and in the homes. This event assists older and newer members to get to know each other.

**A NEW MEMBER CLASS ASSISTS THE ASSIMILATION PROCESS.**
**WHEN** is the best time to teach it?
**WHERE** is the best place to teach it?
**WHO** is the best person to teach it?
**HOW LONG** should the class be?
**WHAT SHOULD BE INCLUDED?**

**WHEN IS THE BEST TIME TO TEACH THE NEW MEMBER CLASS?** Before or after they join the church? Some would call this class a potential new member class if taught before joining the church. Or it could be effectively taught after joining the church. My preference is for anyone who wants to join the church to take the class prior to becoming a member. Sometimes after people join the church, the new member class does not seem to be as effective. New members do not feel it necessary.

**TIME OF THE CLASS:** Our first class was taught during the Sunday School hour. We had 79 in the first class. Teaching it during Sunday school made it easier to encourage people to join a Sunday School class.

Bathroom facilities and a kitchen were available. The number of people in the class would determine the time.

**WHERE:** probably the most effective place would be at the church. This depends upon the number of people in the class and if you provide childcare. If you have small groups, meeting in the homes would be great. Choose a place that would be comfortable and inviting.

**WHO SHOULD BE THE TEACHER?**
In my case the associate pastor taught the class. For me it would be difficult to teach an hour and then lead the worship service right after the class. Of the new members, I discovered a person who loves to teach and I gave him this responsibility the second time. The teacher must be someone the church respects.

**HOW LONG SHOULD THE CLASS BE?**
We very effectively had four one-hour sessions. This schedule allowed for questions and answers. And participants could get to know each other.

**AT THE CONCLUSION:**
We recognized the participants and presented each one with a certificate. At the completion of the class, we presented the people to the church as new members.

**WHAT SHOULD BE INCLUDED IN THE NEW MEMBER CLASS?**

SESSION #1
1. THE PURPOSE AND GOAL OF THE CLASS
2. WHY AM I HERE?
3. HOW TO BE SAVED—admit, believe, accept, invite
4. WHY SHOULD I BE BAPTIZED?
5. WHO SHOULD BE BAPTIZED?
6. WHEN SHOULD I BE BAPTIZED?

SESSION #2
1. OUR PRIORITIES
2. WHAT WE BELIEVE
3. THE ESSENTIALS
4. WHAT WE PRACTICE

SESSION #3
1. OUR PROCEDURES
2. HOW OUR CHURCH IS STRUCTURED
3. DIFFERENCE BETWEEN ATTENDERS AND MEMBERS

SESSION #4: OUR PROCESS
1. THREE FOUNDATIONS OF SPIRITUAL GROWTH
2. IMPORTANT TO BE IN BIBLE STUDY GROUP, SUNDAY SCHOOL

If you want to use this presentation, you may adapt it to your setting.

*These four sessions were contributed by Englewood Baptist Church, Rocky Mount, NC.*

# STEP #7: MOVING OUTWARD / EIGHT OUTREACH MINISTRIES

## DEVELOPING AN OUTWARD FOCUS

The longer a church is declining or plateauing, the harder it becomes to grow and develop an outward focus. As the congregation ages, energy decreases for outreach. Interest declines. Southside had purchased the HWY 97 property to relocate. For ten years, there was no forward progress. They realized they would experience NO GROWTH while they were still located on Church Street. Some still had a bond with the old building and did not want to leave it. After all, it had been good enough for everyone since 1944.

## 1 UPWARD SOCCER

UPWARD SOCCER was the first ministry developed on the new property. Debbie Parker shared that a group was exploring ideas over how they could use the land. Upward Soccer was mentioned.

Debbie Parker called Upward, and they sent a representative to meet with any interested persons. UPWARD offered Southside some money to get started. Church members donated money to buy equipment, goals, and balls. A concession stand was built. The first year 70 children participated. UPWARD SOCCER was successful from the beginning. These directors served all 11 years.

Directors were Debbie Parker, Grace Wallace, Pam Jackson, and Terry Tyson. Many others have helped.

Soccer practiced on Thursday nights and played games on Saturday mornings.

Concessions were available both times. I made it a priority to walk around and talk with all the parents. I made many friends. Generally, of all who participated, one-third were Southside people, one-third were members of other churches, and one-third were not active in any church. Over the past three years, around 100 children accepted Christ, and we baptized many of these.

## ADVERTISING PLAN

We advertised UPWARD SOCCER several ways:
1. Each year we did a mass postcard mailout to 5,000 homes within five miles of the church.
2. We placed 20 yard signs in strategic places in the community.
3. We placed three 4 by 8 banners on the corners of the church property.
4. One thousand postcards were distributed in five local schools. I developed a relationship with school officials. They readily agreed to distribute the cards.
5. We placed six 3 by 4 signs at strategic intersections.
6. The local newspaper offered free listings.
7. We advertised on our LED church sign.

## ATMOSPHERE OF SOCCER FIELDS

Most any Saturday there were upward of 400 people, including grandparents, aunts, uncles, brothers, sisters, and friends, on the soccer fields. At halftime, different people shared a devotion with all present.

CONCESSIONS were a hit. On Thursday nights, in addition to hot dogs and nachos and cheese, there were CHICK-FIL-A sandwiches. On Saturday morning the treat was SAUSAGE DOGS. Families brought lounge chairs. It was just a fun time of fellowship for all ages. Church members often came out and talked to everyone.

I recommend UPWARD to any church looking for a well-organized ministry. UPWARD provides uniforms, trophies, team devotions, and other items. Cost per child varies from year to year. Upward charges $51 per person. In 2016, Southside supplemented $16 per person so the charge per kid became $35. Some kids received scholarships if needed.

**BENEFITS TO THE CHURCH:**
1. Raises community visibility.
2. Enhances church image.
3. Shows that Southside wanted to be a community church.
4. Families often visited the church.
5. Many ministry opportunities resulted.

**UPWARD IS A MINISTRY, NOT A FUND RAISER.**

## 2 TURKEY SHOOT

In the deacons meeting one night, Mike Wall shared how a Turkey Shoot could benefit the church. He said it was a lot of fun and it provided fellowship for the entire family. There was quite a bit of discussion. Finally, the deacons decided that we would do it. Personally I had never been in a church that had a Turkey Shoot. Was it gambling? Fun? Time would tell.

**STEPS FOR GETTING READY FOR THE TURKEY SHOOT**
1. DECIDE THE PURPOSE: It was decided that funds raised would benefit local mission projects.
2. BUILD THE SHOOTING PLATFORM: We needed a flatbed trailer with room for 12 targets. The trailer could be moved at the end of the season.
3. BUILD A SHOOTING STAND: Shooter would lean on the stand to steady their shotgun as they shot.
4. SET THE RULES: Shooters could only use regular 12 gauge guns without any modification. YOUTH could shoot 20 gauge guns.
5. SET THE PRICE PER SHOT: The first few years, the price per shot was $3. With 12 shooting, each round produced $36. In 2016, the price per shot was $4, totaling $48 per round.
6. DECIDE THE PRIZES: CHOICES INCLUDE BACON, COUNTRY HAM, TURKEY, AND SAUSAGE.

**ADVERTISEMENT:**
1. CHURCH SIGN out front of building
2. WORD OF MOUTH
3. CHURCH NEWSLETTER
4. FIVE THOUSAND POSTCARD MAILOUT

**CONCLUSIONS:**
Total money raised for missions:
 2013-2016 $35,000
 2016 $11,000

## 3 OPERATION CHRISTMAS CHILD

Recently, Franklin Graham, executive director of Samaritans Purse, announced that 11,500,000 shoeboxes were given for children all around the world. **SOUTHSIDE PUT TOGETHER 580 SHOEBOXES IN 2016 AND 694 BOXES IN 2017.**

**HOW IT WORKS**
ANYONE CAN DO A SHOEBOX
- SUNDAY SCHOOL CLASSES
- INDIVIDUALS
- CHURCHES

**TOYS:** Include items that children will immediately embrace such as toy cars, yo-yos, jump ropes, balls, toys that light up and make noise (with extra batteries), etc.

**SCHOOL SUPPLIES:** pens, pencils and sharpeners, crayons, markers, notebooks, paper, solar calculators, coloring and picture books, etc.

**ACCESSORIES:** T-shirts, socks, hats, sunglasses, hair clips, jewelry, watches, flashlights (with extra batteries), etc.

**CRAFTS:** Make your own items such as hair bows, finger puppets, and friendship bracelets.

**NON-LIQUID HYGIENE ITEMS:** toothbrushes, bar soap, combs, washcloths, etc.

**VOLUNTEER OPPORTUNITY**
- OCC HEADQUARTERS. Usually in November and December in Boone, they need volunteers to come and help pack the boxes and get them ready to go all around the world. Several of our people went to help.
- LOCAL REGION COLLECTION AREAS. Englewood Baptist Church, Rocky Mount, served as our region collection area. People are always needed at the collection site.

DONORS ARE ENCOURAGED to include a $9 CHECK (2017) to pay for shipping. Collection sites usually start work mid-November. Boxes are shipped around the world in 104 countries.

## 4 DISASTER RELIEF MINISTRY

The goal of the NC BAPTIST MEN is to have a group of trained volunteers who can respond quickly to a disaster.

Periodically, training is offered across the state. Service opportunities include:
- Aviation
- Baptist Educators
- Church Renewal
- Construction
- Disaster Relief
- Family Foundations
- Medical/Dental Van
- Sports
- Partnerships
- Church Programs
- Preparing Meals
- Ramp Building

Of these ministries, Southside was involved with disaster relief, ramp building, and minor home repair.

**SOUTHSIDE'S TEAM HAS RESPONDED TO DISASTERS IN NORTH AND SOUTH CAROLINA.**

**EQUIPMENT NEEDED:** chain saws, hand tools, trailer, van. Volunteers often sleep in churches on air mattresses.

**PROTOCOL:** The local disaster team coordinator will receive a callout from the NC Baptist Convention Disaster Office. Our local coordinator will contact team members to see if and when they can go. Both men and women are needed.

## 5 HANDYMAN MINISTRIES

Every church needs a Handy Man team. Usually there are men and women in every church who are skilled carpenters, roofers, electricians, and painters who can do minor repair. Some of the repair work you might be asked to do:
- Replace missing shingles
- Repair leaky faucets
- Replace broken windows
- Replace light bulbs
- Repair roof
- Install grab bars
- Install smoke detectors
- Replace rotten boards outside and inside the house
- Paint inside rooms
- Yardwork
- Build wheelchair ramps

## 6 BEREAVEMENT MINISTRY

SOUTHSIDE has a very active bereavement team.
GOAL:
1. To see that families have everything they need in the house, including plates, cups, silverware, napkins, ice, and a meal on the day the deceased person dies.
2. A MEAL will be served on the day of the funeral. This may be at the deceased home, the banquet room at the funeral home, or the church.
3. THE TEAM will begin planning the meal for the day of the funeral as soon as the funeral is set.
4. TEAM will determine how many people will be eating.

5. TEAM will call church members for help with providing the food. The church will provide the meat.
6. Normally 35-50 people will eat.
7. PASTOR AND STAFF are always included in the meal.
8. TEAM will set up tables and chairs.
9. TEAM will clean up and put things back where they were.
10. TEAM will prepare a meal for a church member or for someone who lives in the church member's home.

## 7 CHILDREN AND YOUTH MINISTRY

See article written by CJ Cauble
- ACTIVITIES
- BIBLE STUDIES
- MISSION TRAINING
- VACATION BIBLE SCHOOL

## 8 INJOY THRIFT STORE

Local churches in the North Roanoke Baptist Association participate in this ministry. Donations are given by people and are sold in a very attractive store. Profits are given to numerous ministries such as the Pregnancy Care Center, the Homeless Shelter, Peacemakers who minister to inner city familites, and othes. Volunteers help staff INJOY. It is a great ministry.

| 2012 | 200 |
| --- | --- |
| 2013 | 329 |
| 2014 | 381 |
| 2015 | 453 |
| 2016 | 580 |
| 2017 | 694 |

During a business meeting in the summer of 2012 the missions report was being made and Operation Christmas Child was discussed. Having been in charge of this at my prior church, I asked how many boxes the church had been collecting. The response was ABOUT 50. My heart sank. I could have cried. I responded with, "I will do 100 boxes." OCC has been a heartfelt mission for me for about 15 years. Watching the videos of the children and the missionaries who help deliver these boxes will bring a joy that no words can explain. God blesses us each and every day with so much abundance and we are commanded to share with others. I shop year round looking for the best deals with which to fill these boxes. That first year in 2012 we collected 200+ boxes. Each year the number of boxes collected at Southside has increased and with prayers, a lot of asking, and donations from a lot of members, Southside Baptist collected 694 Boxes in 2017. Praise The Lord. (written by Carolyn Varner)

## 2016 UPWARD SOCCER

UPWARD SOCCER DIRECTORS HAVE BEEN FAITHFUL FROM THE BEGINNING—12 YEARS: Debbie Parker, Grace Wallace, Pam Jackson, and Terry Tyson. Many others have been faithful helpers.

**BENEFITS OF UPWARD SOCCER:**
- Christian training for the children
- Time of fellowship for families—up to 400 on soccer fields at one time
- Provided service opportunity for many adult coaches, referees, assistants, and those working the concession stand
- Outreach to the community
- Enhance church image in community

Students from NC Wesleyan College helped with coaching and officiating

Chris and Neal, of Rockstar Magic Ministry, were speakers at the Awards Service several years. These children responded to the invitation accepting Jesus Christ as their Savior.

Almost 100 children accepted Christ during their presentations.

2015 UPWARD SOCCER

## Disaster Relief Ministry

One of my most spiritually fulfilling and uplifting experiences as a Christian has been while serving and helping people who have experienced a devastating loss of personal belongings, a home, and even loved ones due to natural disasters such as flooding or storms. When my wife and I joined Southside in March 2012, the church had just moved to the present location on Highway 97.

Pastor Fowler met with me on several occasions, during which time, a close bond of friendship quickly developed. I shared that I had co-chaired the Disaster Relief Team at my prior church and he asked me if I would consider organizing a team at Southside and serving as the Chairman. After several weeks of prayer, consideration, and discussions with Dr. Fowler and several deacons regarding the challenges involved, we set a plan in motion.

**FIRST**, we needed a group of people to undergo training and be available when natural disasters occur. When the opportunity was offered to the membership, about 25 people responded and were trained during the next few months.

**SECOND**, we needed funding for a 15-passenger van, a 14-foot dual axle utility trailer, and a lot of tools and equipment. There was no money in the fiscal budget for any of this but God placed a burden on the hearts of his people at Southside and things began to happen. Dr. Fowler suggested that I share the need with the church because he believed God would provide, so we did. One of our members donated a vintage Corvette, which was quickly sold to a brother in Christ who is a member of a neighboring church. This, along with another donation, was sufficient to pay for the van. Additional donations were given to purchase the trailer, tools, and supplies, which were needed to equip the trailer. The following year a line item was added to the fiscal budget to provide for ongoing financial needs and each year thereafter. This concludes the highlights of the historical account of the Southside Baptist Church Disaster Relief Team, but this was all set in motion to provide the opportunity to be witnesses for Christ to those in need.

**SUMMARY:** During the past four years we have responded to a number of storms across Eastern North Carolina, providing shoulders to cry on, a listening ear, and volunteers to cut trees off houses, clean debris from driveways/yards, place temporary tarps on roofs, and pray with many people who marveled that there are people who care enough to volunteer and help in times of crisis, refusing to take payment for the help provided, only striving to glorify and lift up the name of Jesus Christ.

**THE FOUR YEARS** I spent at Southside Baptist Church was a very special time in my life, and having moved over a hundred miles away, I deeply miss all my Christian brothers and sisters. —Tom Varner

## Children and Youth Ministry

*By C.J. Cauble, Associate Pastor of Family Ministries*

**THE MINISTRY OF C.J. CAUBLE** was very instrumental in the growth of Southside. He worked tirelessly. I asked him to contribute to this book.

### INTRODUCTION

As I reflect on the children and youth ministries of Southside Baptist from June of 2012 through November of 2016, the phrase, which I have coined when speaking about Southside in general, that comes to mind is: "COME SEE WHAT GOD IS DOING."

I cannot speak to either of these ministries while on Church Street or within the first few months of the move to Carter Road, but I can say that when Shaneki and I came to Southside there was a good foundation of children and youth ministries, as well as students and families, on which to build.

Children and youth ministries are very difficult and rely heavily on the opinion of the parents as to whether or not their child or youth will be involved. I can say that the parents at Southside had and continue to have a strong desire to see their children and youth grow in the Lord.

### CHILDREN'S MINISTRY

The children's ministry at Southside exists for the purpose of introducing children to God the Father, Jesus, the Holy Spirit, and the Bible. It is our prayer that each child will accept Jesus Christ as Savior and Lord and once saved grow in their walk with Him. We accomplish this goal through our Sunday School, Children's Worship, Wednesday nights, and our activities.

**THROUGH SUNDAY SCHOOL** children are introduced to Bible stories and to God through His Word. Our Sunday School is divided by age/grade and is done so by different developmental road marks.

Sunday School also allows children to experience small group and to learn from the Word, the teacher, and each other.

**CHILDREN'S WORSHIP** has gone through a few different revisions. Our current Children's Worship uses the GOSPEL PROJECT to teach children three years old through third grade the Bible in chronological order. It takes about three years to work through the Gospel Project and covers Genesis through Revelation. Children in our Children's Worship will work through the Bible two times if they attend from age three through third grade.

**ON WEDNESDAY NIGHTS**, we offer Mission Friends, Girls in Action (GAs), and Royal Ambassadors (RAs). All three of these groups are sponsored by the Women Missions Union (WMU) and have a focus on international missions and missionaries; home missions and missionaries; and on being a missionary. Southside is a mission minded church and we have it as a priority to teach missions to our children.

**OUR CHILDREN ACTIVITIES** include anything from Vacation Bible School to a trip to a local museum to summer camp to a movie day at the church. Anything that might interest children and parents and can be used to share the gospel is fair game. The children's ministry at Southside is very busy in the summer giving children opportunities to get out and play, but more importantly, to learn more about God. Every activity has a time of Bible study or devotion along with the fun and excitement of whatever we might be doing.

### YOUTH

The purpose of the youth ministry is basically the same. We desire to introduce youth to God so they might be saved and to teach them more about God and His Word. Our prayer is for every youth to accept Christ as Lord and Savior and to grow. We also offer more opportunities for ministry in our ministry. Children do have some outreach opportunities as they go to GAs and RAs, but our youth are older and are given more ministry opportunities.

**SUNDAY SCHOOL:** Our youth enjoy Sunday School, which is a time of small group teaching. They also have an outreach event most Sunday nights called IGNITE. Ignite is a newer part of our youth ministry and is designed to be an outreach event. Each Sunday night has a different theme behind it to give youth something fun to invite their friends to attend. We do a time of devotion at the beginning and then have games and activities. One night was dress pop or dress country. The youth enjoy dressing up, coming for devotion, and then playing games. Ignite is purposely designed to give youth an avenue to invite friends.

**ON WEDNESDAY NIGHTS**, the youth lead worship and have a time of Bible study. This is an amazing time to see youth singing praises to God and to learn more about who God is and who we are in response.

**OUR YOUTH ARE ALSO ACTIVE** through the year. A few of the highlights are the winter retreat, summer camp, Vacation Bible School (VBS), and mission VBS. The winter retreat is a time for youth, and sometimes their families, to go off for the weekend and grow in their own spiritual walk. Summer camp mixes fun, growing personally, and doing missions. While at camp, the youth spend 4-5 hours each day doing missions.

Each morning and night of camp has devotions and Bible study. Summer camp also has fun activities that get youth moving and often thinking about their relationship with the Lord.

**OUR VBS** is a time for our youth to go to VBS and learn about God. They experience VBS as a student. Later in the summer the youth do a mission VBS. While at the mission VBS, the youth become the teachers, and they are fully responsible for all areas of VBS, including opening rally, Bible Study, craft, recreation, music, missions, snack, and closing rally. There have been times one other adult and I were the only adults for a VBS of 20-25. The youth do an amazing job of leading the VBS.

## CONCLUSION

God has truly blessed SOUTHSIDE BAPTIST CHURCH with some amazing families. It is an honor to serve them as the Children and Youth Pastor. I thank God every day for the amazing work He is doing here at Southside. We give Him all the honor, praise, and glory for those who have accepted Jesus Christ as Lord and Savior; for those who have accepted calls to ministry; and for those who are living their lives for Him.

**MISSION VBS.** For four years now our youth have done a VBS at Hickory Baptist Church, located about 15 miles from Southside. Hickory is a small church of about 25 people and could not have VBS

C.J. performs a children's sermon during the AM worship service. He invites all the children to come down. After the sermon, children go to children's church

**60 YOUTH AND ADULTS JUST WENT ON A WINTER RETREAT AT GREAT WOLF LODGE, CONCORD, NC.**

## The Handyman's Ministry

THE HANDYMAN'S MINISTRY is composed of several people, mostly retired men, who have dedicated their talents to the Lord.

This is a group of people who works with their hands and can fix just about anything.

TERRY TYSON LEADS THIS MINISTRY. Terry shares there is never a shortage of men willing to work no matter what the task.

This past year the men have constructed nine wheelchair ramps, and have done minor repairs to several houses and outbuildings.

**WHAT A BLESSING THESE GUYS RECEIVE IN HELPING OTHERS.**

**Terry shared this story:** There was a lady in Wilson who needed a RAMP built, as her husband was coming home from the hospital. She had called several people and could not locate anyone who could help her. She had moved to Wilson from Chicago and did not know anyone to call upon. Someone told her about the Handyman's Ministry. Terry visited and learned that she had the resources to pay for the ramp, she just did not know anyone who could build it. In about six months this lady's father died and they did not need the ramp any longer.

When Terry and some of the men went to take the ramp down, she asked if they knew of anyone who needed some help for Christmas. A family was identified who had lost everything they had in a flood. This mother had two sons who were wheelchair bound. Terry got the sizes and things they wanted for Christmas. The lady from Chicago went shopping and bought for this family. She even bought a Christmas tree with all the decorations.

What an exciting time it was to take these items to the family who was devastated by the flood.

HELPING PEOPLE often brings out the best in people. JESUS SAYS WHEN WE DO FOR OTHERS, WE ARE DOING FOR HIM. This is one of many stories that can be shared.

**One of many ramps our Handyman's Ministry has built.**

# STEP #8: OUTWARD SPECIAL EVENTS

**OUR EXPERIENCE WITH SPECIAL EVENTS:**
- INCREASES ATTENDANCE 25-50 PERCENT.
- INCREASES COMMUNITY VISABILITY
- INCREASES COMMUNITY IMAGE
- CHURCH ENJOYS THEM
- INCREASES VISITOR FLOW
- BUILDS VISITOR DATABASE

**TIPS ON PLANNING SPECIAL EVENTS:**
- Do not plan events too often.
- Plan an event that will be interesting.
- Plan the event well.
- Advertise the event using church newsletters, signs, and mailouts.
- Deliver what you advertise.
- Have a clear goal for each event.
- Register all participants.
- Use door prizes to encourage registration.
- Decide event's target audience.
- Recruit enough volunteers.

**THE POST EVALUATION**
- Were there any surprises?
- Did things go as we planned?
- What would we do different the next time?
- What was best about the event?
- What was worst about the event?
- How could we improve the event?

## 1 THE FALL FESTIVAL

*GOAL: TO PLAN A COMMUNITY EVENT ON OCTOBER 31*

**TARGET GROUP:** Plan an event for the entire family, including:
- Games
- Free food—hot dogs, funnel cakes, fried Oreos, drinks, kettle corn
- Bingo for adults
- Karaoke stage
- Rides—hay ride, horse rides
- Other rides as available
- Train rides
- Multiple door prize drawings for all who register
- Costume contest
- Bounce houses]

**KEYS TO GOOD ATTENDANCE:**
1. We developed a good relationship with several elementary schools both private and public. They will distribute our postcards.
2. Mail a postcard to every house within five miles of the church. Include other events and services on the card.
3. SOUTHSIDE has a LED sign. We start advertising events at least two or three weeks ahead.
4. Attendance has increased each year from 500 the initial year to 3000+- this past year (2017).

2 FIRST RESPONDERS DAY PURPOSE: RECOGNIZE AND HONOR ALL EMT, POLICE, DEPUTY SHERIFFS, FIREMEN, HIGHWAY PATROL, and others who work so hard to keep our communities safe.

**STEP #1: ENLIST PLANNING TEAM**
- Enlist 4-6 on planning team.
- Enlist 4-5 on food team.
- Enlist 3-4 for publicity team.
- Enlist 5-6 for cleanup.
- Decide on food.
- Lunch following the AM service?
- Breakfast of biscuits, sausage, egg, and cheese?
- Decide if food is for first responders or church wide.

**STEP #2: SET DATE AT LEAST 4-6 WEEKS IN ADVANCE.**
- Make a list of all agencies and phone numbers.
- Call each agency asking for representatives from their department.

- THE ROCKY MOUNT FIRE DEPARTMENT brought their color guard and marched into the beginning of the service.

### STEP #3: SECURE SPECIAL SPEAKER FOR THE SERVICE
- Suggestions: the pastor, a fireman, a policeman, or one of the other first responders.

I chose to invite REV. PHIL WIGGINS. In addition to being an ordained minister, Phil serves as CHAPLAIN of the DURHAM Police Department. PHIL also serves as chaplain of the Fraternal Order of Police. He was a great choice as everyone—responders and congregation alike—enjoyed his presentation. Chaplain Wiggins is a personal friend of the pastor.

### STEP #4: EVALUATION
THE DAY WAS EXTREMELY SUCCESSFUL. One responder started attending church as a result of this day. Several shared that the day was really enjoyable.

## 2 FLASHLIGHT EASTER EGGSTRAVAGANZA

**TIME:** For best success, just before Easter
**NEEDED:** 5,000-10,000 pieces of candy
**HELP:** Need as many volunteers as possible
**GETTING READY:**
- Hide the candy and plastic eggs
- Put some prizes in plastic eggs

**OPTIONS:**
- Start movie or games before dark
- Depending upon the number of children, hide the eggs in different sections of the yard
- Divide children into age groups THE FUN STARTS: Find all the eggs using your flashlight.

**RESULTS:** Last year, 300 children attended. We presented the gospel to a large group. We had everyone register and followed up on all prospects.

**ADVERTISING:** We mailed 5,000 postcards to all families living within five miles of the church. This card included other Easter events. We also distributed cards to five area schools.

## 3 SPORTS SUNDAY

**PURPOSE:** Our church is a very sports-minded group. We invited two high school baseball teams to be our guests for the AM service and lunch following. We asked each person if they played any sport to wear their jersey. One team was coached by one of our members. The pastor's two grandchildren played on the other team.

Most of the two teams came along with their coaches and parents.

PASTOR preached a special message, "Life is like a baseball game." It is included in the sermons in the back of this book.

**RESULTS:** We had one of the highest attendances of the year. We ate 500 hot dogs.

## 4 SHOPPING EVENTS

**GOAL:** TO HAVE AN EVENT THAT WOULD INCREASE TRAFFIC FLOW IN OUR CHURCH

**HOW:** Sell spots to vendors. Provide sausage dogs, biscuits. Monies made would benefit a ministry.

**RESULTS:** We raised about $1,000.

## 5 BIKER SUNDAY

THE PLAN:
1. Mike sent invitations to bikers.
2. After church we would ride to Middlesex Children's Home.
3. We collected monetary gifts for Home.
4. Our group cooked lunch for the children. We had a worship service with the children after lunch.
5. One child accepted Christ.

Mike Wall suggested to me that we have a Biker Sunday.

# Sports Sunday • May 15 10:45

**Many of our youth play sports. Please wear your uniforms this day.**

**Menu:**
**Hamburgers, Hot Dogs**

# WE HONOR OUR EMS/FIRST RESPONDERS
# OUR UNSUNG HEROES
# JANUARY 25  10:45 AM

We at Southside Baptist Church realize that everyday you put your life on the line to keep our community safe.

- We want to honor you and your families for your service.
- We want to show support for all EMS/ law enforcement both locally and across the country
- We want to honor those men and women who gave the ultimate sacrifice

Our special speaker is Rev Phil Wiggins of Durham. Phil served on the Durham Police Force for many years. Since 1983, he has served as chaplain of the Durham PD. Also Phil has been on staff at Summit Church for 10 years and is minister of Pastoral Care & Senior Adults. He serves as chaplain of the Fraternal Order of Police and is active as state chaplain.

PHIL is a friend of our pastor.

### REV. PHIL WIGGINS
## EVERYONE WELCOME!

## SCHEDULE
## JANUARY 25
## 10:00 AM

- coffee & juice
- sausage biscuits
- Donuts & pastries

## 10:45 AM

# SOUTHSIDE BAPTIST CHURCH
4948 CARTER ROAD    NEXT TO L&L   HWY 97   JUST PAST RWI
## THANK YOU FOR ALL YOU DO

Some of the First Responders who attended

# Fall Carnival

**A FALL FESTIVAL WILL**
- Raise Community Awareness
- Increase Church Visitor Flow
- Increase Visitor Data Base
- Create Community Goodwill
- Provide Good Christian Fun

**HORSE RIDES**
**PHOTO BOOTH**
**CARNIVAL RIDES**
**GAMES**
**KARAOKE**
**BOUNCIES**
**KETTLE CORN**
**FUNNEL CAKES**
**DRINKS**
**HOT DOGS**
**BINGO**
**DOOR PRIZES**

## THE FALL FESTIVAL
### by Rose Fowler Griffin

I was the Chairman of the SPECIAL EVENTS COMMITTEE for several years. Our emphasis was outreach to the community. The biggest event is the FALL FESTIVAL. We had 1,500 people our first year and 2,000-3,000 in additional years. There was no guide to follow so we worked by trial and error. I'd like to share some things that we learned and points to consider.

**ISSUES TO ANSWER:**
   What is our budget?
   Date for the festival?
   How will we advertise?
   What is our goal?
   How to follow-up?
   How to share gospel?
   What type of activities to have?

**BUDGET:** Southside had money in the budget for the Fall Festival—first year was $600.

**OUR BUDGET INCREASED EACH YEAR:** In 2016, we had $4,800. After the success of the first year, we were able to gradually increase the budget to include items such as lights, bounce houses, pony rides, and small amusements rides.

**ACTIVITIES:**
**TRUNK-A-TREAT, GAMES, AND A HAYRIDE.**
Church people were slow to volunteer to sign up for trunks because they had never seen it before. We showed some pictures from the Internet in church as examples. We also asked for candy donations. It is better to set a candy goal. Generally, for a crowd of 1,000 people, you need 10,000 pieces of candy. After the first year, we organized a board and asked for specific types of candy so we didn't get all of a specific type such as all chocolate.

**DATE: OCTOBER 31—HALLOWEEN.**
If the goal is to reach un-churched people, then you go where they are. They are out on Halloween. They must have a reason to need to fill out the registration card or they won't do it. Also think about the most strategic places to have your registration tables. You will need several locations. Most parents want a safe, fun place to take their children and that is what we offered. In return, we distributed information about VBS, Upward Sports, Christmas activities, and general information about our church.

**REGISTRATION:** We needed a way to capture names, addresses, phone numbers, email addresses, etc., so we could follow up with the contacts. Each person was asked to fill out a registration card for door prizes.

**DOOR PRIZES:** We asked LOCAL restaurants such as Pizza Inn, local burger places, and retail stores to donate door prizes. For the grand prize, we bought a $100 GIFT CARD from the budget.

**ADVERTISING:** We mailed a POSTCARD with the Fall Festival dates and other church activities to all homes within five miles of the church. Five thousand postcards would cost about $400 and saturation mailing would cost eight cents each. This mailing would reach the community at a lower mailing cost DISTRIBUTE POSTCARDS TO FIVE AREA LOCAL SCHOOLS.

BANNERS were used in several locations around the community advertising the event.

**FOLLOW UP WITH UNCHURCHED:**
Monthly church newsletters were mailed to each family for three months. Sometimes personal visits were made.

**SALVATION BRACELETS:** A craft booth was set up to make salvation bracelets and explain the plan of Salvation. We had four salvations our first year. The Salvation Bracelets would have the colors red, black, white, green, and yellow.
   **Red—The blood of Christ**
   **Black—Sin**

White—Forgiveness
Green—Growing as a Christian
Yellow—Heaven

Bible stories on the hayride were really effective. The second year, it didn't work as well with the bracelets so we regrouped. Both the parents and children were captive audiences!

**CANDY:** At every game and booth, children got candy. We also had a person that was the "MC." That person played music, pulled names for the door prizes, and kept the "party" going. He frequently mentioned church activities coming up and encouraged people to sign up for door prizes and the big grand prize.

**BINGO**

ACTIVITIES were fun! We started with Trunk-a-Treat and games. A lady in our congregation had a ranch so she brought her horses for HORSE RIDES. We had games for kids two and up. Our older adults are very active and come to all the events, so we had BINGO! That was a big hit.

We went to the local thrift store and bought mugs and other trinkets as prizes. In the next years, as the budget grew, we were able to add some small amusement rides such as a train pulled by a lawn mower. We tried having the games inside the church but found that most of the crowd stayed outside so we transitioned everything outside after the first year.

**FOOD!!** Since our focus is on outreach, we felt everything should be FREE. We didn't charge for drinks or food. We bought drinks for a month when they were on sale. Our menu was basic: hot dogs, chips, drinks, and kettle corn. One of our members made funnel cakes and fried Oreos.

### THE ATMOSPHERE WAS LIKE A CARNIVAL.

# STEP #9: OUTWARD MISSIONS

**NINETY PERCENT OF ALL CHURCHES ARE NOT GROWING BECAUSE THEY ARE INWARD FOCUSED.**
- The longer a church is the same size the less likely it will grow.
- Most churches reach their current size within the first 15 years.
- It is easier to give money to missions than to be involved in missions.
- You can look at today's bulletin and nothing has changed in the last 30 years.
- **DO THE SAME THINGS, GET THE SAME RESULTS.**

**TO EXPERIENCE REVITALIZATION:**
- Inward focus must turn outward.
- Church must become more missional in purpose.
- Church must see people as Jesus saw them, as sheep without a shepherd.
- New members must be assimilated.

**HOW DO YOU DO THIS?**
LEAD people to become involved in hands-on missions.
- LOCAL
- STATE
- NATIONAL
- INTERNATIONAL

**WARNING: CAN'T DO IT OVERNIGHT.**

## LOCAL MISSIONS:

**HANDYMAN'S MINISTRY:** A group of men and women were interested in doing minor home repairs for people who could not afford to pay. Leaky faucets, rotten steps, holes in walls and ceilings, and broken windows were some of the repair jobs.

**RAMP BUILDERS:** We have built numerous handicap ramps in the community. Sometimes the church pays for all the materials. Sometimes the recipient pays for the materials as we furnish the labor.

**VOLUNTEERING AT INJOY:** Injoy is a thrift store sponsored by our local Baptist Association. Volunteers process donations as they come in and display items for sale. All profits support missions.

**MISSION VACATION BIBLE SCHOOL:** For five years, our youth have assisted a local church in doing VBS. This church would have been unable to do the VBS alone. We have shared our materials with many others.

**FALL FESTIVAL:** Held on Halloween, this event is the biggest of the year. In 2016, 3,000 attended. Five hundred registered, indicating they were not involved in any church. While the event was happening, we had a team of people sharing the gospel with whomever would listen. For several years we used the Salvation Bracelet.

**SPECIAL DAYS:** BIKER SUNDAY was an enjoyable day. Fifteen bikers attended and after church rode to the Middlesex Children's Home for lunch with the residents. We took them a monetary gift. The gospel was presented.

## STATE AND NATIONAL MISSIONS:

**YOUTH** have participated in MissionFuge for several years. This is sponsored by Lifeway of the Southern Baptist Convention. Youth attend Bible studies in the mornings, participate in local missions in the afternoon, and have worship services at night. This is held in various locations.

**YOUTH AND ADULTS** have been on mission trips in New York, Kentucky, and West Virginia. They have assisted churches in Vacation Bible School and Outreach.

## INTERNATIONAL MISSIONS:

Kelsey Murray has served in UGANDA while in college. Missionaries speak regularly.

**MISSIONS HELPS CHURCHES TO TURN AROUND.**
- GIVING AND DOING FOR OTHERS PRODUCES GREAT RESULTS IN ONE'S SPIRITUAL DEVELOPMENT.

**SUGGESTION:**
- Once per quarter Southside has a mission report night.
- Share pictures and testimonies.
- Put pictures and events in church newsletter

> **PROOF OF REVITALIZATION**
> All ages are excited about ministry. YOUTH help in inner city Rocky Mount with a Bible School. They do several mission projects each year. YOUNG ADULTS go annually to West Virginia. They visit the Middlesex Children's Home. ADULTS are involved with Disaster Relief, ramp building, home repair, Injoy, special events, VBS, working with children and youth.
>
> **ANSWER CALL TO MINISTRY**
> Several people in our church have felt that God was leading them into ministry.

**JC COATS** has served on staff for the past two summers. Southside licensed him to the gospel ministry. He has completed two years at North Greenville Univ. He plans to go to seminary after completing college.

**LESLEY MURRAY** has served this past year as Youth Minister. She has finished her first year teaching school and plans to attend Southeastern Seminary part time. She has done an outstanding job among us.

**DREW JOHNSON** feels that God has led him into ministry. He left Southside to move to Alabama, where he served as youth minister.

**THIS FINE GROUP OF YOUNG ADULTS** have been going to Webster Springs, WV, since they were teens. Now in their twenties, they have numerous responsibilities in the church. Sunday School Director, Sunday School teachers, Deacon, small group leaders, youth minister, and usher. They love the Lord and have a deep desire to SERVE.

**JON KEEL** has served for several summers at Camp Willow Run, a Christian camp. He has literally touched thousands of lives. He works with summer camps and weekend retreats. Jon now serves full time with this ministry.

**MEET JONATHAN AND BECCA PIFER:** Jonathan served on our staff for eight months as Minister of Discipleship and Outreach while finishing his studies at Southeastern Seminary. Becca served as our church secretary. Jonathan grew up in Ecuador, the son of missionaries. He and Becca feel the call to return to Ecuador to serve as full-time missionaries and are in the process of raising their funds.

# STEP #10: GETTING OUT THE WORD

**TWO CHALLENGES:**
1. How did we notify the community of the first service on March 4, 2012?
2. How did we effectively follow-up visitors after the first service?

**STEP #1: PRAY**

God honors hard work and planning in getting ready for this exciting day.

**STEP #2: USE AVAILABLE MEDIA**
- People ride by and see construction —7,000 cars go by the church daily.
- Church has been under construction for nine months.
- Visible signs.
- Mass mail.
- Word of mouth.
- Newspaper notification.
- The church newsletter.

I was the only full-time staff person when we had our first Sunday. We began this media presence when our associate pastor came on board three and a half months later. We did have a part-time secretary who worked 9 AM-1 PM each day.

**STEP #3: DEVELOP MEDIA PRESENCE**

**WEBPAGE:** Many people will look at the Church's webpage before they decide to visit a church. Pages need to be attractive, informative, and updated regularly. Past sermons, upcoming activities, and pictures of past activities will gain the attention of the viewer. Our associate pastor came on board three months after the first Sunday. Media was his responsibility. COST is inexpensive.

**FACEBOOK:** FB has improved so much. You can GO LIVE and broadcast messages, make announcements, develop group of friends who like your page, send announcements. FB can reach literally hundreds if not thousands.

**EMAILS:** Continually building your DATABASE is a must. We try to register all participants to our events and ministries. Names go into our database. Members, visitors, and anyone who has an interest in your church should be included. Using the EXCEL spreadsheet in the Microsoft Office Package is my recommendation. It is easy to generate MAILING LABELS, as DATA transfers into other programs easily.

**PHONE CALLS:** There are several services to choose from.

**SERVICE #1:** would input numbers, make messages, and broadcast one number at the time. It would take three hours to transmit 350 numbers. You purchase the machine and optional support.

**SERVICE #2:** Put numbers in, make messages, and send it to all numbers at the same time. It is easy to send messages from your smart phone at any location. You pay an annual fee depending upon your phone number count.

## The Church Newsletter

**THE CHURCH NEWSLETTER** can be a great advertising tool to your church's ministries and events each month. My suggestions:
- Use 11.5 x 17 paper.
- Do full color on both sides.
- Use the front panel for upcoming events.
- Use the inside for pastors and/or staff articles.
- Include many pictures from the past month's events and ministries.
- Use lower back page for address label, return address, postal permit, picture of the church.
- Use upper back page for average attendances, new members, announcements, reminders, special offerings.
- Take pictures of everything you do, include new members.
- Microsoft Publisher is easy to use to set up the newsletter. Most printers have this available to them.

**NEWSLETTER DISTRIBUTION:**
- **POSTAL MAILING:** Send to mailing list. You must send at least 200 to use the BULK MAILING PERMIT. Cost as of this printing is about 18 cents each.
- **ELECTRONIC MAILING:** For everyone for whom you have their email address, and who have chosen to get their newsletter electronically, you can send it for nothing and save 18 cents.

**GROW YOUR DATABASE:**
**FROM SPECIAL EVENTS**
- Register all visitors.
- We offer DOOR PRIZES and gift cards. Local restaurants will supply freebies for advertisement.
- **FALL FESTIVAL:** Out of 3,000 attenders, usually 500 are unchurched.
- **VBS:** Out of 250 attenders, about 20 percent are unchurched.
- **UPWARD SOCCER:** Of 100 players, about one-third are unchurched.
- **EASTER EGGRAVAGANZA:** About 15-20 percent of attenders are unchurched.

**MAILING FREQUENCY:**
- We FOUND that mailing to prospects for at least six months produces more results than just one month.
- **DATABASE:** Be sure and note at what event the prospect attended and the date. This will help you to delete some off the list.
- INFO ALSO APPLIES to postcards.

**THINGS TO REMEMBER:**
- PRINT A TOP QUALITY NEWSLETTER OR MAILOUT.
- Using a professional printer gives better results than a copy machine.
- REMEMBER: People often make a decision to visit or not visit when they see your printed piece.

## How to Mail for Less Than Ten Cents Each

**STEP #1: CHOOSE YOUR MAILING FROM THESE THREE OPTIONS**
1. FIRST CLASS STAMP—requires a postage stamp, name, and address affixed to each newsletter.
2. BULK MAIL—is the most economical way to mail the newsletter. Bulk mail saves a lot of money. Bulk mail permit requires mailing at least 200 copies. Postage is about 18 cents each. Mailing the newsletter requires a complete address.
3. SATURATION MAIL: Saturation mail in when you mail to every address on a carrier route. Most carrier routes average 600-625 addresses each. Saturation mail is when you saturate the carrier route with your piece. Every home/ business gets one. Postage is about 8 cents per piece. This is used successfully if you mail to everyone within five miles of the church or specified carrier routes.

**STEP #2: PURCHASE A NON- PROFIT MAILING PERMIT**

You can apply for a non-profit permit at the local post office. An annual fee varies each year. For 2017 the fee was $275. A bulk mail permit is required for SATURATION MAIL AND BULK MAIL.

**STEP #3: CHOOSE MAILING AREA**

The easiest way to choose your mailing area is to follow these directions:
1. https://eddm.usps.com/eddm/customer/ route. Search.actionUS Postal Service/Every Door Direct Mail.
2. Type in your address: For example, 4948 Carter Road, Elm City, NC 27822.
3. Click search. You will see a red emblem that pinpoints your location.
4. Change radius to desired distance— for my mailout, I chose five miles.
5. Hover over the location with the mouse and you will see various carrier routes.

| Zip Code | Carrier Route | Addesses |
|----------|---------------|----------|
| 27803    | RRO12         | 695      |
| 27822    | RR092         | 621      |
| 27822    | RR094         | 662      |
| 27822    | RR091         | 651      |
| 27896    | R0001         | 609      |
| TOTAL PIECES |           | 3238     |

### STEP #4: ANSWER THESE QUESTIONS

1. What events do you want to advertise? Events should be within 30-45 days.
2. Who is my target group? Age? Where do they live?
3. Will my event be of interest to my target group?
4. What geographical area do I want to penetrate?

## Preparing the Mailout

### STEP #1: SELECT MAILOUT SIZE

I have used two sizes of mailouts effectively.

1. 5.5x8.5 gives more space to advertise multiple events.
2. 4x6 is better for advertising one or two events. See samples of both sizes of mailouts at the end of this chapter.

### STEP #2: DESIGN MAILOUT TO ADVERTISE YOUR EVENTS

1. VACATION BIBLE SCHOOL: Usually planned during the summer, VBS always attracts children. Dates should be well advertised three weeks in advance. Also children and youth activities are regularly planned along with camps, mission trips, mission VBS, and retreats. The mailout should include all these events.
2. UPWARD SPORTS and any other summer or fall activities: For the past two years, we have planned guest speakers, films, and musical groups on Sunday nights.
3. CHRISTMAS EVENTS: The Christmas play, musical programs, mission emphasis, Christmas birthday party, food baskets for those needing a blessing, Samaritan Purse Shoeboxes.
4. EASTER lends itself to have a community Easter Egg Hunt. A successful event is the flashlight Easter Egg Hunt after dark. Food, fun, fellowship always are an attraction. You may include multiple events on one card.

### STEP #3: CHOOSE FREQUENCY OF MAILOUTS

- A periodic MAILOUT can enhance your church's ministry if well done and targeted properly.
- Some of the mailouts that cross my desk are poorly done and portray a bad image of the church.
- The mailout should give the reader a view of the activities and ministries of the church.
- It should contain exciting details of the events that it is promoting. Often the reader makes a decision whether to visit or not to visit your church while viewing the mailout.

### STEP #4: ESTIMATE THE COST

Within five miles of Southside Baptist Church there are 3,238 addresses, multiplied by eight cents equals $259.40.

Printing cost averages between five and seven cents per piece depending upon size, 4x6 or 6x8, and whether it's full color and/or both sides.

A good place to get an estimate is US PRESS. COM: 800 227-7377. We use a local printer most of the time and return time is usually faster than US Press. US Press does good work and I highly recommend them. Paul Briggs is one of the customer reps and will be glad to assist you.

### STEP #5: GET MAILOUT PRINTED YOU MAY WANT TO GET TWO OR THREE ESTIMATES.

### STEP #6 CHOOSE DISTRIBUTION

1. SATURATION MAIL—we mail to all 3,500 homes within five miles of the church.

2. LOCAL SCHOOL DISTRIBUTION: While at Southside, I have developed relationships with several schools both Christian and public. Our church is blessed with many school teachers. They help distribute our mailout to all the students. Between these schools, we distribute to 1,800. NO POSTAGE IS INVOLVED with these. Also, local convenience stores will let you put signs and cards in their stores.

## WHAT RESULTS CAN I EXPECT FROM MASS MAILOUT AND DISTRIBUTION?

The purpose of the mailouts/mass distributions:
1. Builds the church's image in the community.
2. Increases your visitor flow to the events and to your church.
3. It is important to capture names, addresses, and email at your events.
4. Follow-up mailouts are important—I recommend at least four per year.
5. The third mailout brings more results that the first or second.

**Homes within a 5 mile radius of the church**

### ON EDDM Website:
1. Pinpoint your church location by inserting your address.
2. Type in THE RADIUS you want to reach from one mile to five miles.
3. Select the carrier routes. Each route has 600+/- addresses. Totals show up on right side. Disregard the price.
4. Saturation mail is around eight cents per piece.
5. Get the bulk mail office at the Post Office to show you how to label each route.
6. You may select other areas to mail.

## WE WORSHIP - WE SERVE - WE FELLOWSHIP

InJoy reports sales have surpassed $1,000,000 the first 16 months

### CHURCH STAFF

| | |
|---|---|
| Pastor | Dr Harry Fowler |
| Associate Pastor | Rev. C.J. Cauble |
| Worship Leader | Danny Daughtridge |

### NEW MEMBER'S CLASS
### DISCOVERING SOUTHSIDE
Taught by CJ Cauble

EASTER SUNRISE

### WELCOME NEW MEMBERS
Carysn Edwards

### AVERAGES FOR FEBRUARY
| | |
|---|---|
| SUNDAY SCHOOL | 143 |
| MORNING WORSHIP | 200 |
| SUN. NIGHT WORSHIP | 72 |

### ATTENTION ENERGIZERS
Going to Spring Time Jubilee in Myrtle Beach April 27-29. Events—Preaching, singing,

### COMING IN OCTOBER
- UPWARD SOCCER
- CONTINUES
- SPECIAL EVENTS
- OCT 8

SOUTHERN BAPTIST world hunger FUND

### NEEDED FOR FALL FESTIVAL
### OCTOBER 31
### 6:30– 8:30

The special events team is gearing up for our FIFTH Fall Festival, to be held Monday, October 31

### SEPTEMBER & OCTOBER MISSIONS

- Many of our men and women support and pray for those having surgery—wheelchair RAMPS

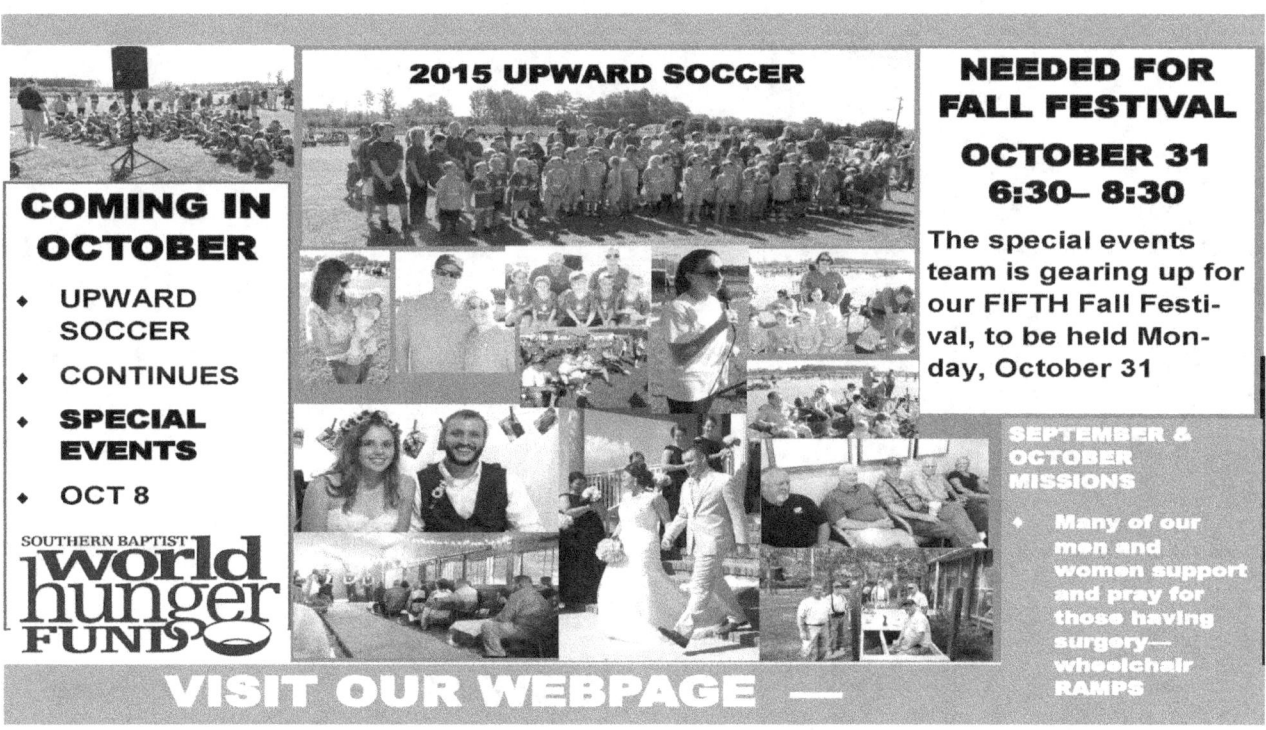

VISIT OUR WEBPAGE

# OCTOBER 2016
## Southside BAPTIST CHURCH

## OCTOBER

**DR. ROBIN FISHER**    **REV JAMES ROGERSON**    **OCTOBER**    **REV WALT COOPER**

**DR WRAY WHEELESS** — **WEST MOUNT BAPTIST**

**GOAL 500** — NOV 4-5

## FIRST NIGHT

**FRIDAY & SATURDAY nights 7-9 PM**

**SOUTHSIDE BAPTIST CHURCH**
proceeds Southside mission projects

## FALL FESTIVAL

**Trunk or Treat**

HOT DOGS

CANDY

FUNNEL

## ALL AGES

## WE WORSHIP - WE SERVE - WE FELLOWSHIP

**CHURCH STAFF**

| | |
|---|---|
| Pastor | Dr Harry Fowler |
| Associate Pastor | Rev. C.J. Cauble |
| Secretary | Suzette Evans |
| Interim Music | Tammy & Darryl |

**RECENT HAT DAY IN HONOR OF DARENDA PROCTOR**

Darenda was recently diagnosed with breast cancer. She has begun chemo treatment. She got a special

**DECEMBER AVERAGES**

| | |
|---|---|
| SUNDAY SCHOOL | 136 |
| MORNING WORSHIP | 202 |
| SUN. NIGHT WORSHIP | 118 |

**WEDNESDAY NIGHT SCHEDULE**

6:00 PM ADULT CHOIR REHERSAL

7:00 RA'S, GA'S, YOUTH

**LOTTIE MOON OFFERING**

**GOAL $ 5,000**

**GIVEN $5,759**

**UPCOMING EVENTS**

- JAN 31 SONG SERVICE
- FEB 13 VALENTINE BANQUET
- FEB 14 WOMEN ON MISSION DAY

## WE WORSHIP - WE SERVE - WE FELLOWSHIP

**CHURCH STAFF**

| | |
|---|---|
| pastor | Dr Harry Fowler |
| Associate Pastor | Rev. C.J. Cauble |
| Worship Leader | Danny |

**WELCOME NEW MEMBERS**

Carysn Edwards

**AVERAGES FOR JANUARY**

| | |
|---|---|
| SUNDAY SCHOOL | 131 |
| AM WORSHIP | 230 |

**MAY 2015**

# Southside BAPTIST CHURCH

## Church YARD SALE

**YARD SALE**

Saturday June 6

7:00am-12:00pm

$20 for 2 Parks/spaces

### FAMILY MOVIE NIGHT

**WHEN THE GAME STANDS TALL**

MAY 17  5:30-

**BBQ and Chicken Plate Sale**

Pick up 11:00 am until 2:00 pm

Delivery with

**GARDNER'S**

Proceeds benefit a mission trip to New York

## Friday, May 22nd

# OUR CHURCH SPEAKS

*BY BOBBY CLAY LONGTIME MEMBER, DEACON, SUNDAY SCHOOL TEACHER*

I have been a member of Southside since 1979. I accepted the Lord as my Savior in 1961.

OVER THE YEARS, I served the Lord at Southside in many positions: Sunday school teacher, trustee, deacon, Long Range Planning Committee, and director.

**SINCE RELOCATING:**

I don't think I have ever seen the blessings from the Lord before like I have felt during our building and relocation. I have been humbled and blessed to be a part of what happened. Our membership had dwindled to about fifty or sixty people at the former location. We only had about five or six youth left. We were afraid we wouldn't be able to build the new church, and we didn't for about ten years. Why? Because the Lord wasn't ready for us to build at that time. Then God sent Dr. Fowler and his family to lead us, and everything fell into place.

WE BUILT the new church and were concerned about paying for it. Then GOD SENT NEW MEMBERS to us. From all over the area, God sent people to help. God blessed us in a way that I had never experienced before, AND I WAS AND STILL AM HUMBLED BY IT. YOU SEE, GOD HAD A PLAN. Our plans didn't work until God was ready. It's such a blessing that all of OUR MEMBERS HAVE BLENDED INTO ONE.

We at Southside have a bond and love for each other through our Lord and Savior Jesus Christ. God has blessed us with GREAT LEADERSHIP in our church. Leaders who aren't concerned about "self." To take the gospel to all people and minister to the poor, we must decrease for God to increase.

**BY MARVIN STALLINGS**

*NEW MEMBER, DEACON, SUNDAY SCHOOL TEACHER*

Thank you, SOUTHSIDE, for taking *THE LEAP OF FAITH* that has blessed so many of us that came later.

- We thank you, Lord, for sending the pastor our church needed, with vision, faith, encouragement, and knowledge to implement *The Leap of Faith*.
- Thank you, Dr. Fowler, for being the pastor we needed.

Dr. Fowler told us he and the church had been praying hard for God to send the workers that were needed, and our group was an answer to their prayers. Dr. Harry Fowler and Terry Tyson met with us and assured us that they needed us and they personally welcomed each one of us to be a member of Southside. God's spirit moved in our hearts, bringing peace and direction that He wanted us to be a part of Southside Baptist Church.

In the following months, WE CAME FORWARD IN WAVES to join the church. We were graciously received and were given opportunity to serve.

Words cannot describe how wonderful our membership at Southside has been. Jesus' love is what binds us together. The fruit of that love is the tremendous growth in the number of people in the community that are being saved and becoming members of Southside. They now are the largest people group in the triangle. The beauty is Jesus has made the three groups one. Galatians 3:28 says, "There is neither Jew nor Greek, there is neither bond nor free, there is neither male nor female: for ye are all one in Christ Jesus" (KJV). Amen. GOD BLESS YOU, DR. FOWLER, FOR WRITING THIS BOOK ON WHAT GOD HAS DONE AND IS DOING AT SOUTHSIDE BAPTIST CHURCH. TO GOD BE ALL PRAISE AND GLORY.

**BY JERRY CALHOUN**

*CHARTER MEMBER*

When the church split and so many of my friends left, I was very low. One morning while reading my devotion, the Scripture read, "separate yourself from this congregation." I felt that the Lord was telling me to leave Southside. I told my husband this and he said, "The Lord has not told me to go anywhere."

My mother was up in age and had been at Southside since the beginning and I knew this would upset her to go to another church. So I prayed hard and stayed. NOW I AM SO GLAD I DID AND HAVE LIVED TO SEE THE GREAT THINGS GOD HAS DONE IN SOUTHSIDE.

**BY LESLEY MURRAY**
*FIVE YEARS AS YOUTH LEADER*

> He is no fool who gives what he cannot keep to gain that which he cannot lose. –Jim Elliot

God has strategically placed you where you are for a purpose and that purpose is to show the gospel in all you do.

Sometimes with words, other times with actions. And sometimes, it's simply being a friend, getting coffee together and talking about life together. It rarely looks the same. Sometimes it's getting phone calls at midnight from one of your high school youth girls about boy trouble. Ministry for each person looks different but it has one common theme: loving God, and in turn, loving and serving others well.

**"Wherever you are, be all there." –Jim Elliot, American missionary and martyr**

The summer after graduation from college, I worked as the summer intern for children and youth. The growth and passion for the Lord I saw in the lives of the young people at church were fantastic. I knew after finishing up for the summer, I wanted to continue being involved with the youth program. There was not at that time a youth program on Sunday nights for them to attend. After seeing the need, I decided to start a program called IGNITE.

- Ignite nights are outreach focused and meant to be high energy, fun activities to attract young people.
- The goal is to make it easier to invite non-believers or unchurched friends to study the Bible together while fellowshipping in a fun activity.
- It is important to meet the youth where they are in life and talk about real things that they struggle with.
- The goal of Ignite is to build Christian community in which we can use to the Bible to figure out what it means to be unashamed of the gospel and live boldly for Jesus Christ.
- I want the events to keep them interested in coming while being high energy and fun.
- Some of these events range from paint slip-n-slide, to camo scavenger hunts, relay races, movie nights, praise and worship nights, tie dye events, 'Merica nights, and more.

IGNITE would not be possible without the tremendous help and support of the young adult Sunday school class. They serve the Lord and the ministry sacrificially with not just their time, but financially and letting us use their homes for events.

To help build community, we also started having GIRLS' AND GUYS' NIGHTS that meet outside of church at people's home once a month. For the girls, this looks like carving pumpkins on a Friday night, playing hide and seek for hours, and taco bars. The girls have also had a Pancakes and pajamas night in which everyone wore pajamas, ate one too many pancakes, played games, and watched a movie. THE GUYS' NIGHTS look a little bit different. More "manly," if you will. The guys' nights have included bonfires, cookouts, playing football and basketball, and hanging out.

*"Do not be conformed to this world, but be transformed by the renewal of your mind, that by testing you may discern what is the will of God, what is good and acceptable and perfect." (Romans 12:2, ESV)*

God is moving in the lives of the young people at Southside Baptist and it is a pleasure to get to be a part. I am thankful to Southside for the opportunity to help lead the youth activities. WHILE MINISTRY IS NEVER AN EASY JOB, IT HAS AN ETERNAL IMPACT. Daily choosing to serve the Lord is not an easy path, but there is none more satisfying.

## BY LINDA WILLIAMS

*MEMBER FOR FIVE YEARS, SUNDAY SCHOOL TEACHER, PIANIST, MISSIONS LEADER, SERVES ON VARIOUS COMMITTEES*

It is truly amazing how God gives us what we need when we need it. Jeremiah 29:11 sums it up perfectly with a message from the Lord: "'For I know the plans I have for you,' declares the LORD, 'plans to prosper you and not harm you, plans to give you hope and a future'" (NIV). I came to Southside's new church building aching from a church split. I walked into the building that first Sunday in March trying to be invisible, trying to blend in, longing to worship—truly worship—with fellow believers. Before I was even able to enter the Worship Center, a gentleman in black greeted me with open arms and asked me my name. Little did I know that my effort to "slip in" was futile. My greeter was the pastor himself, Dr. Fowler!

For many previous years, I had driven by the property on Highway 97 pondering why on earth a church would be built in this location with so many churches in the community. Little did I know that this church building was being built for me! I had watched the land being cleared, the soccer being played, the Vacation Bible School happenings, and finally the building was ready for worship. God was preparing the community for His church. He was preparing me. The Scripture in Jeremiah continues with the following promise: "'Then you will call on me and come and pray to me, and I will listen to you. You will seek me and find me when you seek me with all your heart. I will be found by you,' declares the LORD" (29:12-14, NIV). As I prayed for guidance, I found the place God wanted me to grow and serve at Southside.

I often call Southside the CHURCH OF SECOND CHANCES. So many people from so many places and experiences have come to be part of the Southside family. Dr. Fowler worked tirelessly to unite, to get to know the different people, and to learn the different strengths for service. Under his leadership, the church grew rapidly. It has become a family that will love you no matter what. Southside is a band of believers upon which you can call, cry, hug, and rejoice. I have learned through this experience that a church isn't a building. It is the people, God's people. God's love is the foundation upon which He builds His church, His people. Our sole purpose is to glorify Him.

## BY GAIL MASON

*SIX YEARS AS SUNDAY SCHOOL TEACHER, NURSERY AND CHILDREN'S CHURCH VOLUNTEER*

Our first visit at Southside was the beginning of a new journey for our family. We had never felt such devotional love from a church family and the interim pastor, Dr. Harry Fowler. As we entered through the doors of that church when it was still located on Church Street, we could feel the genuine kindness and love offered within those walls. By the second Sunday, we were ready to call Southside our home. Southside is where my son Jake said his first public prayer to the congregation during a children's sermon, at the ripe young age of three. It is where both my son and daughter, Emily, have accepted Jesus Christ as their Lord and Savior, and where they were baptized. It is where my husband and I have been teaching Sunday school for the past six years. Southside will continue to be our holy home, because God filled it with such wonderful people who embrace serving Him, in the community, and anywhere else God may call them to go.

## BY MIKE AND TAMMY WALL

*MIKE'S FUNERAL WAS HELD AT SOUTHSIDE ON APRIL 24, 2017; HE WAS A DEACON, AND ALSO PROPOSED TO THE DEACONS TO BEGIN THE TURKEY SHOOT*

**WHAT SOUTHSIDE HAS MEANT TO ME:**

Southside means to me a place of worship for my whole family and a place to help me continue my walk with the Lord. By my coming to Southside, my whole family has joined. My daughter Tiffany, husband Brandon, and twins Cheyenne and Brayden were baptized. I baptized my grandson Brayden. Southside is a loving church for each person who walks through the door.

## BY CHARLIE LONG
*SUNDAY SCHOOL TEACHER, DEACON, SERVED ON VARIOUS COMMITTEES*
**WHAT SERVING OF DEACON HAS MEANT TO ME:**
Looking back on 40+ years of serving, I feel somewhat humbled and blessed. I have experienced so many great relationships through deacon ministry. My wife passed away March 19, 1999, after a short battle with cancer. The love and support of my church family was unbelievable.

I have learned over the years the importance of staying connected to Christ and His people. Through deacon ministry you have the opportunity to make a difference in people's lives. People may not remember what you said but they will remember that you were there. Never underestimate the importance of presence (God and yours). Southside has experienced many changes in the last seven years. God changed our location, sent new workers, added new ministries, guided in two building programs.

---

> Having been a member for 43 years, I think the best is yet to come. God is good all the time.

---

## BY SANDY VICKERS
When I came in the first Sunday, six people hugged me. I will never forget that day. The church was so warm and friendly. It was also the day I joined. There were 19 of us. What a day!

## BY GRACE WALLACE
Served on Long Range Planning Committee. Member of Southside all her life.

Having grown up attending Southside Baptist Church I was excited and honored to serve on the Long Range Planning Committee. Members of the church dreamed for so long to build on the land we had purchased. Often I heard older members say, "It will never happen in my lifetime," and hearing that statement was disheartening! In order to survive, and not close the doors as many predicted, the Long Range Planning Committee knew we had to relocate. There were a lot of ups and downs during the planning process.

Probably the hardest thing we faced was convincing the members we had to STEP OUT ON FAITH and begin the building process, even if our current building had not sold. After many hours and sometimes stressful meetings, we had a building plan and it was presented to the church. What an awesome feeling it was when the vote was unanimous to move forward with our building plans.

Proverbs 3:5-6 says, "Trust in the LORD with all your heart and lean not on your own understanding; in all your ways submit to him, and he will make your paths straight" (NIV). Stepping out on faith, we did just that. We trusted in the Lord and look what we have to show for our FAITH! I am very thankful to all who served on the Long Range Planning Committee and other members of the church who supported us during this phase of our church. I look forward to how God will use each one of us in the future.

## BY JOHNNY AND JOYCE IPOCK
Johnny is one of our newer deacons. For a number of years, we were members of a large church. Although it was a great group of people and a wonderful church, we found it difficult to plug into ways to serve. Since we both grew up in small churches, we began to feel the need to find a new church home. We watched as Southside was being constructed and felt we should visit; after all, it was only five minutes from home.

A few months after Southside opened its new doors, we decided it was time for us to visit. The minute we walked in, we were made to feel welcomed. Everyone was so friendly and the atmosphere was warm and inviting . . . it far exceeded our expectations. We both quickly found areas where we could serve. I love to cook, so becoming a part of the once-a-month family night dinners was great and Johnny joined the disaster relief team, as well as helping out where needed. We know one reason God put Southside in their new location was so we could have a loving church family and find opportunities to better serve Him.

## BY CHRIS AND CRYSTAL WOOD

Crystal is my niece. She had been trying to get pregnant. One day at church they asked me to have the church pray for them that they would get pregnant. They came to the altar. Both sat at the front and deacons and leaders came and laid hands on them and prayed that she would get pregnant. In a few weeks Crystal announced to the church that she was pregnant. The audience clapped and praised the Lord. After she became pregnant many ladies in the church asked me not to pray for them.

My husband and I were led to Southside on the first Sunday in their new building. We had been out of church for some time and were looking for a church to be a part of. It only took one Sunday to know this was where we belonged. I enjoyed hearing my Uncle Harry preach, and everyone welcomed us into their church family. Little did we know how special this church would be to us.

My husband and I had been married for many years and struggled with not being able to have children. I would often question God as to why I couldn't have a baby. I now know that God always has a perfect plan in His timing. We just have to be patient and have faith.

In January of 2014, Chris and I decided to take a leap of faith and try in-vitro fertilization. We knew this would be a difficult process and would need many prayers. I decided one Sunday to go before the church and ask everyone to please pray for us to have a baby. I told myself that if this were God's plan it would happen. A few weeks later, we found out our procedure was successful and that I was pregnant. Fast-forward nearly four years later, we have a healthy son, Collin, a gift from God made possible through the thoughts, prayers, and blessing of Southside Baptist Church.

## BY JC COATS

JC and his mother, Beth, came to Southside a few years ago. While in high school, he recognized that God was calling him into the ministry.

I had the privilege of spending two summers at Southside in 2016 and 2017. In the summer of 2016, I was looking for a church internship so I could gain experience for Christian Studies, which is what I am currently studying at North Greenville University in Greenville, SC. Dr. Fowler kindly offered me to work with him that summer and I accepted. Under Dr. Fowler, I spent a lot of time doing visits and outreach. From Dr. Fowler, I learned how important it is to love people inside and outside of your church.

The following summer (2017), Rev. C.J. Cauble invited me back to be one of the church's summer missionaries. In both of these summers, I have grown exponentially in my walk with the Lord and my calling to ministry. Southside holds a special place in my heart in my training for ministry. I was licensed there and was mentored by some great people with a passion for the Lord. I am thankful for the opportunity to be a part of what God has done at Southside.

# THIS PAGE DEDICATED TO MIKE WALL

**FROM PASTOR FOWLER:**

I first met MIKE WALL at the funeral of Tinny Johnson. He and Tammy were pulling him to the cemetery.

Afterward Mike and Tammy started coming to Southside. Before long their daughter Tiffany and family started attending. I baptized Tiffany, Brandon, and Cheyenne. Mike baptized Brayden.

- Mike was ordained a deacon.
- He proposed to the deacons to begin the Turkey Shoot.

**THE STREETS OF GOLD HEARSE CO**

is a ministry that God led him to start.

- He built the hearse.
- He served many funerals.
- Bikers use his service.
- Often used for servicemen killed in action.
- MIKE, YOU AND TAMMY HAVE MADE A DIFFERENCE IN THIS WORLD. I HAVE ENJOYED BEING YOUR PASTOR. I LOVE Y'ALL VERY MUCH. I AM SO GLAD OUR PATHS CROSSED ALONG THE WAY.

## MIKE, THANKS FOR YOUR SERVICE TO THE LORD.

# RESOURCES

# LEADING SOMEONE TO CHRIST (all Scripture KJV)

## FACT #1: GOD HAS A GIFT FOR YOU

*JOHN 3:16*
For God so loved the world, that he gave his only begotten Son, that whosoever believeth in him should not perish, but have everlasting life.

## FACT #2: WE ARE SINNERS

*ROMANS 3:23*
For all have sinned, and come short of the glory of God.

## FACT #3: GOD JUDGES SIN

*ROMANS 6:23*
For the wages of sin is death; but the gift of God is eternal life through Jesus Christ our Lord.

## FACT #4: JESUS DIED FOR US

*MATTHEW 20:28*
Even as the Son of man came not to be ministered unto, but to minister, and to give his life a ransom for many.

## FACT #5: JESUS BUILT A BRIDGE TO HEAVEN

*JOHN 14:6*
Jesus saith unto him, I am the way, the truth, and the life: no man cometh unto the Father, but by me.

## FACT #6: HOW TO RECEIVE THIS GIFT

*ACTS 16:31*
And they said, Believe on the Lord Jesus Christ, and thou shalt be saved, and thy house.

*ROMANS 10:9*
That if thou shalt confess with thy mouth the Lord Jesus, and shalt believe in thine heart that God hath raised him from the dead, thou shalt be saved.

## FACT #7: AFTER YOU HAVE ACCEPTED CHRIST INTO YOUR HEART

*ACTS 22:16*
And now why tarriest thou? arise, and be baptized, and wash away thy sins, calling on the name of the Lord.

*MATTHEW 3:17*
And lo a voice from heaven, saying, This is my beloved Son, in whom I am well pleased.

## FACT #8: READ THE BIBLE, PRAY, AND GO TO CHURCH

# 5 MOTIVATIONAL SERMONS

## Ditches in the Desert, 2 Kings 3 (KJV)

### WHEN GOD SHOWS UP THE UNUSUAL BECOMES USUAL

*THE ALLIANCE*

1: JEHORAM, son of Ahab, KING over Israel in Samaria, put away the pillar of Baal that his parents made, but clung to the sin of Jeroboam. HE LED ISRAEL TO SIN.

3: JEHORAM cleaved to the sins of his father.

4: MESHA, KING OF MOAB and sheep breeder, had to deliver animals to the King of Israel due to past losing battle. Annually delivered these animals:
- 100,000 lambs
- 100,000 rams with wool

5: AHAB died; King of Moab rebelled, DID NOT WANT TO PAY ANYMORE.

6: King JEHORAM went out of Samaria.

7: Called for JESHOPHAT of Judah to help him—will you go into battle with me?

8: Which way are we going? Through the wilderness of Edom.

9: Israel, Judah, Edom journeyed seven days. ENCOUNTERED HUGE PROBLEM—NO WATER. WHAT DO YOU DO WHEN YOU ENCOUNTER A BIG ROADBLOCK?

### GET THE PREACHER

11: WANTED TO FIND A PROPHET TO INQUIRE OF THE LORD.

When things are going smooth, you do not need a preacher; when things get tough, you DO. ELISHA was the successor to ELIJAH. KINGS went to see what Elisha would tell them.

13: ELISHA'S RESPONSE: Why come to see me?
- To iquire of your father's prophets.

THE PROBLEM: NO WATER FOR HORSES, MEN, CATTLE. They had traveled for seven days; they were hot, tired, out of water—desperate.

### ELISHA'S RESPONSE

16: Make valley full of ditches.

10: Saw impossible task IN DRY DESERT, chose to march south to Desert of Edom, half-circle pattern to surprise attack.

### SEVEN-DAY ATTACK, NO WATER

10: Johoram blamed the Lord—no water, he was terrified, caused panic attack. Officer informed kings about Elisha, prophet who succeeded Elijah.

13-14 Joram rebuked.

### DESPERATE SITUATION

- Often find self in dry desert spiritually.
- Seems like not as close to God as you used to be.
- GOD HAS NOT MOVED—YOU HAVE.
- Neglect reading of the WORD.
- Quit serving HIM.
- Quit going to CHURCH.
- Many Christians are spiritual babes.

15: BRING ME A MINSTREL THE PLACE OF MUSIC

The minstrel played, GOD'S hand fell upon ELISHA.

### GET READY FOR THE BLESSING DIG A DITCH

*2 Kings 3:16-17 (KJV)*
*And he said, Thus saith the LORD, Make this valley full of ditches. For thus saith the LORD, Ye shall not see wind, neither shall ye see rain; yet that valley shall be filled with water, that ye may drink, both ye, and your cattle, and your beasts.*

WHERE DOES RAIN COME FROM? NO WIND, NO RAIN, BUT VALLEY WILL BE FULL. NOW GOD DOES HIS PART. MAN MUST DO HIS PART. MAN'S PART IS TO DIG THE DITCHES. TWO MIRACLES ABOUT TO BE PERFORMED.

1. God will flood valley full of water for you, your cattle, and your beasts.

2. God will give victory over Moab. 19: God will destroy food, cities, water supply, can't resettle.
20: Water came by way of Edom.

## MOAB SAW RED WATER WHEN SUN CAME UP.
He saw water in the ditches and thought it was blood; he thought coalition army had killed themselves.

## MAIN POINTS
1. It's not our fullness that attracts God, it's our emptiness.
2. It's not our strength that touches God, it's our weakness.
3. It's not our dignity that impresses God, it's our desperation.

- IT IS WAS AN EASY THING in the eyes of the Lord to create the heavens and the earth.
- IT WAS AN EASY THING in the eyes of the Lord to have the creativity to create so many different and unique and beautiful creatures.
- IT WAS AN EASY THING in the eyes of the Lord to provide for three million people in a desert for 40 years.
- IT WAS AN EASY THING in the eyes of the Lord to deliver Israel time and time again against outnumbered and outgunned nations.
- IT WAS AN EASY THING in the eyes of the Lord to heal the many sicknesses told about in the Bible.
- IT WAS AN EASY THING in the eyes of the Lord to cause a virgin to be pregnant and to be pregnant with One who was divine and human.
- IT WAS AN EASY THING in the eyes of the Lord to raise Jesus from the dead.
- IT WILL BE AN EASY THING in the eyes of the Lord to completely and forever defeat Satan and all his hosts.
- IT WILL BE AN EASY THING in the eyes of the Lord to create a new heavens and a new earth.

## GOD SPECIALIZES IN FILLING THINGS WHICH ARE EMPTY.
ILL Augustine (AD 354-430) said, "God wants to give us something, but cannot, because our hands are full—there's nowhere for him to put it." **When we feel as though God's blessings are missing from our lives, we need to examine our hands and see if they are open to receive, or clutched around something that we refuse to let go.**

## FAITH DETERMINES THE LEVEL OF BLESSINGS
*BUT GOD'S PLAN FOR THEM AND FOR US REQUIRES A RESPONSE.*
They had to get busy and dig ditches in the valley. They had to participate and they had to have the faith that God would provide, or they would have never dug the ditches.

## 16: MAKE VALLEY FULL OF DITCHES
17: NO WIND, NO RAIN—valley full of water.
18: GOD will deliver MOAB into your hands.

## GOD TESTS OUR TRUST AND FAITH IN HIM
- These men did what God had told them to do.
- They did something that may have sounded foolish, but they were obedient.
- When they did this, God supplied them with more water than they needed.
- God filled these ditches with water.
- He did this with His supernatural power.

## GOD'S POWER ALWAYS EXCEEDS OUR EXPECTATIONS.
Verses 21-24
- Moabites saw red water, thought blood bath.
- Water confused Moabites but refreshed Israel.
- God handed victory over to three kings.
- Moab defeated with very little effort.
- Hardest thing to do was to dig the ditches.

*GOD WILL GIVE YOU MORE THAN YOU ASK FOR.*

20: THEY WORSHIPPED—spiritually prepared. God inhabits praise of man.

**PEOPLE GAVE THEIR OFFERING.**
- Flood gates opened.
- Country filled with water.
- Only limited by the ditches they dug.

FIRST their thirst was satisfied, and then they went on to smite the Moabites, even into their own country. And so it is, that when we bring our emptiness to God he fills us, and satisfies the cry of our hearts, and then He empowers us to go forth and conquer every enemy of our souls.

He used the water to confuse the Moabites. You see, the Moabites knew that there was NO WATER down in that valley, and when they woke up that morning, they looked out, and the Bible says that the sun shone red on the water and it looked like blood.

The Moabites thought that there had been a blood bath, they thought that the three kings had fought against each other and destroyed each other, and they ran in to get all the spoils and plunder. But they had another thing coming. You see, God had confused them.

God had made the sun to reflect off of the water just right and the Moabites thought that it was the blood of the opposing army.

God had handed the battle over to the three kings. What did they want? WATER
What did they get? WATER AND VICTORY.

**GOD'S POWER ALWAYS EXCEEDS OUR EXPECTATIONS.**

God had allowed the Moabites to be defeated with very little effort.

My brother Ron had a dog named Lucy. She often would bury all the food Ron gave her, and one time she buried the bowl along with the food. She didn't realize that as long as she belonged to Ron, she would be fed. WE OFTEN HOARD WHAT GOD GIVES US TODAY BECAUSE WE DON'T TRUST HIM TO PROVIDE FOR OUR NEEDS TOMORROW. The difference one person can make often seems minuscule in comparison with the need at hand, but what you're doing may make a big difference in the life and eternity of one person.

MESSAGE TO SOUTHSIDE:
- WE believe that God wants us to relocate.
- GOD will do HIS part.
- WE must do OUR part.
- INSTRUCTIONS may sound silly and stupid.
- GOD WILL BLESS us according to our faith.

**LORD, GIVE ME A BIGGER SHOVEL.**

---

The hardest thing this army had to do was dig the ditches. God did the rest.

---

## Rich Young Ruler, Mark 10:17-25 (KJV)

17: Jesus going about the day.
- One came running to Jesus.
- Man knelt down, today we'd call him a SEEKER.
- Matthew 7:7-8 (KJV)
  *Ask, and it shall be given you; seek, and ye shall find; knock, and it shall be opened unto you: For every one that asketh receiveth; and he THAT SEEKETH findeth; and to him that knocketh it shall be opened.*
- Isaiah 55:6-7 (KJV)
  *SEEK ye the LORD while he may be found, call ye upon him while he is near: Let the wicked forsake his way, and the unrighteous man his thoughts: and let him return unto the LORD, and he will have mercy upon him; and to our God, for he will abundantly pardon.*

**THE QUESTION:**
*WHAT CAN I DO TO INHERIT ETERNAL LIFE?*
- He realized a need in his life.
- He knew Jesus was a man of God, a GOOD MASTER.

JESUS' ANSWER: answered question with a question.
- Why do you call me good?
- You know the commandments—adultery, kill, steal, bear false witness, honor father and mother.

RYR'S RESPONSE:
- Master, done all of these since my youth.

JESUS' RESPONSE:
- JESUS loved him.
- *ONE THING THOU LACK.*
- Can't go to heaven by being good.
- Can't work your way into heaven.
- ONE THING YOU LACK: V. 21. YOUR WEALTH IN HEAVEN.

*WHAT YOU HAVE TO DO:*
- Sell what you have.
- Give to the poor—PAY AHEAD.
- Shall have treasures in heaven.
- Take up your cross and follow me.

RICH YOUNG RULER'S RESPONSE:
- Grieved, had great possessions.
- Not willing to pay the price.

JESUS TAKES OPPORTUNITY FOR TEACHING MOMENT WITH DISCIPLES.
- Hard for one with riches to enter heaven.
- V. 24: repeated, hard for rich to trust God.
- Easier for camel to go through the eye of a needle than rich to get into heaven.

## WHAT WE LEARN ABOUT THE RICH YOUNG RULER

HE was not willing to pay the price.
GOOD POINTS
- Wealthy.
- Young, many years before him.
- Eager.
- Morally clean.
- Religious but lost.
- Humble—he knelt.
- He had courage—ran to Jesus.
- GOOD SENSE—went to right place, seeking the right thing, at the right time.
- He was seeking to know more.
- He realized the need in his life.
- He kept the law.
- He showed discernment as he knelt.
- He was willing to learn and listen.
- He had great potential.
- He SEEMED to be disciple in the making.

## MISTAKES
- He did not accept Jesus and offer to follow Him.
- He went away—did not stay, refused to follow Jesus.

## THINGS TO LEARN
- Spiritual things cannot be satisfied by fame, fortune.
- Opportunities do not last forever.
- There are defining moments that once past are past.
- Acts 24:25 (KJV)
  And as he reasoned of righteousness, temperance, and judgment to come,

FELIX trembled, and answered, Go thy way for this time; when I have a CONVENIENT season, I will call for thee.
- Acts 26:28 (KJV)
  Then AGRIPPA said unto Paul, Almost thou persuadest me to be a Christian.
- Lacked willingness to put Christ above all else.
- Loved his gold.
- One thing—alcohol, drugs, sex, fame, lust, popularity.
- He left heaven when he left Jesus.

*Mark 8:36 (KJV)*
*What shall it profit a man, if he shall gain the whole world, and lose his own soul?*

## IN CLOSING—

Look at what he was offered. He was offered a Savior who would save his soul. He was offered a cross that would lead to a crown. He was offered a home in heaven. Look at what he refused. He refused it all.

## MONEY IS YOUR BARRIER

*Matthew 16:25 (KJV)*
*For whosoever will save his life shall lose it: but whosoever will lose his life for my sake shall find it.*

*Matthew 6:20-21 (KJV)*
*But lay up for yourselves treasures in heaven, where neither moth nor rust doth corrupt, and where thieves do not break through nor steal: For where your treasure is, there will your heart be also.*

# Decision Time

## TRUTHS DR. FOWLER TAUGHT US

*SOUTHSIDE IS AT A CRITICAL POINT*
TWO CHOICES: DIE OR MOVE FORWARD
SOUTHSIDE IS AT STAGE 6 OF THE LIFE CYCLE.

Joshua and the children of Israel had reached the Jordan River and there was no way to cross. They had wandered in the wilderness for 40 years. They were punished because of their lack of faith when the twelve spies went into the Promised Land. Ten spies said there was no way Israel could take the Promised Land. The people were like giants. Two spies said they could do it.

JOSHUA and CALEB were the only positive thinkers of the twelve.

1. GOD CAN SELL THE BUILDING when it is time to move. Southside had been depending on themselves and not on God.
2. THE TEN SPIES COULD NOT SEE A WAY to move across the Jordan and take Jericho. The people were so much BIGGER and STRONGER than they were.
3. After 40 years in the wilderness, where most of them died because of their lack of faith, Joshua was told by God it was time to MOVE. Israel had faith that they could cross the Jordan because GOD WOULD MAKE A WAY TO CROSS THE JORDAN RIVER.
4. Southside could build and relocate because GOD WOULD MAKE A WAY if the people believed and had faith.
5. Through this process God would show the people WHO were in charge and teach them to depend on HIM.
6. When the priests put their foot into the water, then the Jordan parted.

## ANOTHER BIBLICAL TRUTH

Israel had lived in Egypt for 400 years. God called MOSES to lead the people to the PROMISED LAND.

*Exodus 14:15-17 (KJV)*
*And the LORD said unto Moses, Wherefore criest thou unto me? speak unto the children of Israel, THAT THEY GO FORWARD: But lift thou up thy rod, and stretch out thine hand over the sea, and divide it: and the children of Israel shall go on dry ground through the midst of the sea. And I, behold, I will harden the hearts of the Egyptians, and they shall follow them: and I will get me honuor upon Pharaoh, and upon all his host, upon his chariots, and upon his horsemen.*

After a time of inactivity, GOD SAID IT WAS TIME TO MOVE FORWARD.

---

### DR. FOWLER'S NOTE:
This was a relatively easy decision.
- The bottom line people did not want to die and see the church close.
- They were comfortable with the loan.
- They were ready to take the Leap of Faith.
- They felt it was God's time.
- They knew this would probably be their last opportunity.

**TIME TO DECIDE YES OR NO. SOUTHSIDE SAID LET'S DO IT.**

They had wandered in the wilderness for 40 years. They were punished because their lack of faith when the twelve spies went into the Promised Land. Ten said there was no way Israel could take the Promised Land. The people were like giants. Two spies said they could do it. JOSHUA and CALEB were the only positive thinkers of the twelve.

**PREPARATIONS FOR THE MOVE**
- ARRANGE FOR THE FINANCING.
- DRAW AND APPROVE BUILDING PLANS.
- PREPARE FOR NEW MEMBERS.
- MAKE NECESSARY CHANGES IN WAY WE DID THINGS.
- MINISTRY ADJUSTMENTS.
- LEADERSHIP ADJUSTMENTS.
- DR. FOWLER'S 12 RECOMMENDATIONS.

**QUESTIONS:**
- WILL WE HAVE NEW MEMBERS?
- HOW MANY CAN WE EXPECT?
- WILL BE ABLE TO REPAY THE LOAN?
- WE DON'T HAVE ENOUGH CHILD AND YOUTH LEADERS NOW.
- WHERE WILL LEADERS COME FROM?
- THERE ARE SO MANY UNKNOWNS.

**HIGHWAY TRAFFIC**

NCDOT tells us that 7,000 cars travel by our property every day.

**UNDERSTANDING THE HARVEST**

*GETTING READY FOR THE HARVEST*

> *Matthew 9:37-38 (KJV)*
> *Then saith he unto his disciples, The harvest truly is plenteous, but the labourers are few; Pray ye therefore the Lord of the harvest, that he will send forth labourers into his harvest.*

PRAY for laborers

When many of our people thought about working in the harvest, the first thing they thought about was going door to door in the new community. One person said they had gone door to door in the past in the current community with minimum results.

**IDENTIFYING THE HARVEST**
- MUST study the demographics of the church ministry area.
- Learned there are 14,000 people who live within five miles of the new location.
- If Southside is going to be successful, we must reach young families with youth children.
- Not enough laborers available to accomplish this; therefore, we MUST PRAY FOR LABORERS.
- Southside had a successful UPWARD SOCCER program for several years. Most of the families who participated were young and had young children. THREE basic groups participated: some were Southside members, some were active members of other churches, and some were unchurched.
- I put together a rather simple questionnaire asking the soccer parents to help me. Among other things I asked this question: If you were looking for a church, what would you look for? What advice could you give me as pastor? Most responses were geared to a church having a strong children's ministry.

---

**If We Continue Doing What We Have Been Doing, Then We Can Expect the Same Results.**

---

**OUR SITUATION:**

All ages were welcome. But our target group would be young families with children. We had several adults who worked with children. But if we had an influx of people, we would not have enough laborers to help us. If we had a big influx and could not produce a good nursery, children, and youth program, then we would be in worse shape than before we moved. There were NO babies in the nursery on Church Street.

- My thoughts: Where would these people come from?
- Would they come back?
- Would they help us with developing children and youth classes?
- Would they help us teach Sunday school?
- Would they provide tithes and offerings to help pay the bills?

## Life Is like a Game of Baseball

### BASEBALL AND LIFE HAVE NO CLOCK.
- ONLY SPORT THAT HAS NO TIME CLOCK.
- DO NOT KNOW HOW LONG IT LASTS.
- No time limit or "sudden death" overtime.
- THERE IS AN END BUT DON'T KNOW WHEN.
- Other day 20 strikeouts— probably short game.
- LIFE IS LIKE THAT.
- SOME die young and others live long.

*Matthew 6:34 (KJV)*
*Take therefore no thought for the morrow: for the morrow shall take thought for the things of itself. Sufficient unto the day is the evil thereof.*

### JUST BECAUSE YOU ARE AHEAD NOW DOES NOT MEAN YOU WIN.
Whoever is ahead at the end will win. HEARD about a team that got behind 20-0 . . . but they had not come up to the plate yet.

*Matthew 24:13 (KJV)*
*But he that shall endure unto the end, the same shall be saved.*

### ALL MAKE MISTAKES/ERRORS.

*Romans 3:23 (KJV)*
*For all have sinned, and come short of the glory of God.*

*Romans 3:10 (KJV)*
*As it is written, There is none righteous, no, not one.*

- Throw to wrong base
- Drop the ball
- Overthrow the ball
- Misjudge the ball
- Swing at a bad pitch

### SOME DAYS NOTHING GOES RIGHT.
- SAY wrong thing
- DO wrong thing
- Can't catch
- Can't hit

### GAME IS A SERIES OF BALLS/STRIKES.
- During nine innings you should get four at bats, and you get four balls and three strikes and a whole bunch of foul balls.
- Last batter to hit 400 was Ted Williams in 1941.
- Home runs: Barry Bonds 762, Hank Aaron 755, Babe Ruth 714.
- Babe Ruth struck out 1,330 times.
- In baseball, like life, you get multiple chances to succeed.
- When you strike out, DON'T GET DISCOURAGED.
- DON'T QUIT.

### BASEBALL REQUIRES TEAMWORK.
- Like life, you can't excel individually.
- Double play normally takes 2 or 3 players.
- *GENESIS 2:18 (KJV)*
  *And the LORD God said, It is not good that the man should be alone; I will make him an help meet for him.*
- Created for community.

### BASEBALL SOMETIMES REQUIRES SACRIFICES FOR THE GOOD OF THE TEAM.
- In baseball, like life, we are sometimes asked to make sacrifices for the good of the group.

- In baseball the sacrifice bunt is used to advance the runners.
- A sacrifice fly with less than two outs can score a runner from third base.
- STEAL a base to get into a better position.
- *EXODUS 20:15 (KJV)*
  *Thou shalt not steal.*
- Unlike life, umpires are exposed to stealing quite often. Stealing bases is not only OK, but encouraged in baseball.

## UMPIRES
- CALL IT LIKE THEY SEE IT.
- Baseball's policemen are the umpires.
- SOMETIMES GET CALLS WRONG.

## GAME IS A LEARNING PROCESS
- Life is a learning process
- We can learn some things from the game of baseball.

1- We're on a team, so be a team player.
2- We have a coach, so listen to Him and do your best.
3- Have good attitude

LL.- Some of you may remember that baseball player LOU GEHRIG is called the "iron man of baseball" for a very good reason. For 15 years in the 1920s and 30s he played first base for the New York Yankees. He played 2,130 consecutive games. And after he retired they X-rayed both of his hands and found that every finger had been broken at least one time, YET HE NEVER MISSED A GAME! He played even though he was hurt. That says something about his character.

TY COBB, considered by many to be the greatest ballplayer of all time, played 3,033 games and for 12 years led the American League in batting average. For four years, he batted over 400.

On his deathbed, July 17, 1961, at the age of 74 years, he accepted Jesus Christ as his Savior. He said, "You tell the boys I'm sorry it was the last part of the ninth that I came to know Christ. I wish it had taken place in the first half of the first."

JACKIE ROBINSON was the first African American to play baseball in the major leagues. Breaking baseball's color barrier, he faced hostile crowds in every stadium. While playing one day in his home stadium of Ebbets Field in Brooklyn, he committed an error. The fans began to jeer him. He stood at second base, humiliated, while up the crowd booed. Then, without saying a word, shortstop Pee Wee Reese went over and stood next to Jackie. He put his arm around him and faced the crowd. Suddenly the fans grew quiet. Robinson later said that arm around his shoulder saved his career.

## BASEBALL IN HEAVEN
Bob and Stan were good buddies and baseball friends. One day at a ballgame, they made a vow to each other that, whichever friend died first, that friend would send a message back to earth to let the other friend know if there was baseball in heaven.

Sure enough, one day Bob died. After a while, he sent a message back to earth to Stan: "Hey, Stan, this is your old baseball buddy, Bob. I have good news and I have bad news for you from heaven."

Stan thought about it and said, "Let's hear the good news!" Bob said, "Well, the good news is there is a lot of baseball going on in heaven! Mickey Mantle is hitting home runs a mile long and you should see Babe Ruth hit a baseball up here, too! It really is baseball heaven!"

Stan smiled and said, "Hey, Bob. What about that bad news?"

There was a long pause. Finally, Bob spoke from heaven and said, "The bad news is, YOU ARE SCHEDULED TO PITCH UP HERE TOMORROW NIGHT!"

https://www.youtube.com/watch?v=- K3DI07Ibb4

# Move Forward, Deuteronomy 1:6

> **PURPOSE: FAILING TO MOVE FORWARD** cost the Israelites 40 extra years. The negative people never realized the dream.

## 11-DAY JOURNEY FROM EGYPT TO PROMISED LAND TURNED INTO A 40-YEAR EXPERIENCE— HAD TO LEARN SOME LESSONS

AT THE EDGE of the Promised Land
- In a holding pattern
- Had to make a decision
- Easy to become satisfied

## OBSTACLES ALONG THE WAY:
*NO FOOD*

*Exodus 16:35 (KJV)*
*And the children of Israel did eat manna forty years, until they came to a land inhabited; they did eat manna, until they came unto the borders of the land of Canaan.*

- Rather die in Egypt a slave that starve out here.
- *Numbers 20:4-5 (MSG)*
  *Why did you haul this congregation of GOD out here into this wilderness to die, people and cattle alike? And why did you take us out of Egypt in the first place, dragging us into this miserable country? NO GRAIN, NO FIGS, NO GRAPEVINES, NO POMEGRANATES— AND NOW NOT EVEN ANY WATER!*

*NO WATER*

*Numbers 20:11 (MSG)*
*With that Moses raised his arm and slammed his staff against the rock—once, twice. Water poured out. Congregation and cattle drank.*

## MOSES WAS PUNISHED

*Deuteronomy 3:26-27 (MSG)*
*But GOD was still angry with me because of you. He wouldn't listen. He said, "Enough of that. Not another word from you on this. Climb to the top of Mount Pisgah and look around: look west, north, south, east. Take in the land with your own eyes. Take a good look because you're not going to cross this Jordan.*

## NEGATIVE ATTITUDE—WE CAN'T DO IT
*THE REPORT*

*Numbers 13:31-33 (MSG)*
*But the others said, "We can't attack those people; THEY'RE WAY STRONGER THAN WE ARE." They spread scary rumors among the People of Israel. They said, "We scouted out the land from one end to the other—it's a land that swallows people whole.*
*EVERYBODY WE SAW WAS HUGE.*
*WHY, WE EVEN SAW THE NEPHILIM GIANTS (the Anak giants come from the Nephilim). Alongside them we felt like grasshoppers. And they looked down on us as if we were GRASSHOPPERS."*

## ISRAEL'S MANY EXPERIENCES
- JOURNEYS
- CHALLENGES
- TRANSITIONS
- ABRAHAM MOVED FROM UR TO CANAAN
- JOSEPH SOLD INTO SLAVERY IN EGYPT
- MOSES – 12 PLAGUES
- THE RED SEA
- JOSHUA
  AMAZING – LOOK WHAT GOD HAS DONE THROUGH IT ALL
- GOD BLESSED

## THE BEST IS YET TO COME

*Deuteronomy 1:6 (KJV)*
The lord our god spake unto us in horeb, saying, ye have dwelt long enough in this mount.

## TIME TO MOVE OUT AND MOVE FORWARD

*Deuteronomy 1:8 (MSG)*
Look, I've given you this land. Now go in and take it. It's the land GOD promised to give your ancestors Abraham, Isaac, and Jacob and their children after them.

*Exodus 14:14-16 (KJV)*
THE LORD SHALL FIGHT FOR YOU, and ye shall hold your peace.
And the LORD said unto Moses,
Wherefore criest thou unto me? speak unto the children of Israel,
THAT THEY GO FORWARD:
But lift thou up thy rod, and stretch out thine hand over the sea, and divide it: and the children of Israel shall go on dry ground through the midst of the sea.

## WHEN GOD SAYS IT'S TIME, MOVE OUT AND MOVE FORWARD.

### ALL KIND OF EXCUSES
- Many have excuses why they can't do it now.

### PARABLE OF THE GREAT SUPPER –
Persons invited had manyExcuses:
- Went and bought a field.
- Check out the five oxen.
- Took a wife – had to be with her.

**SOMETIMES WE MISS WHAT GOD HAS FOR US BECAUSE WHEN GOD CALLS WE ARE NOT READY.**

**DURING MANY AN INVITATION, GOD WILL TELL YOU TO COME TO THE ALTAR AND PRAY AND YOU ARE JUST SIMPLY NOT READY.**

**WHEN WAS THE LAST TIME YOU WERE NOT READY WHEN GOD CALLED?**

# 10 BIBLICAL GROWTH KEYS

## KEY #1:

*THE MINISTRY OF THE HOLY SPIRIT PROVIDED THE POWER FOR CHURCH GROWTH.*

A. THE HOLY SPIRIT CONVICTS
   1. John 12:32 — DRAWS
   2. Acts 2:37 — PRICKS
   3. John 16:8 — REPROVES

B. THE HOLY SPIRIT SAVES
   1. John 3:16 — GAVE JESUS
   2. Romans 10:13 — WHO SO EVER

C. THE HOLY SPIRIT EMPOWERS THE BELIEVER
   1. Acts 1:8 power to — WITNESS
   2. Luke 10:19 power to — OVERCOME ENEMY

D. THE HOLY SPIRIT EQUIPS THE BELIEVER
   1. I Corinthians 12:6 — PURPOSE
   2. Ephesians 4:12 — SPIRITUAL GIFTS

***PRINCIPLE: The holy spirit provides the basis and power for church growth. Churches grow as they honor the presence of the holy spirit.***

## KEY #2:

*GOD CHOSE MAN TO BE A MEMBER OF THE LEADERSHIP TEAM*

A. GOD IS THE HEAD OF THE LEADERSHIP TEAM
   1. Colossians 1:18 — HEAD OF BODY
   2. I Corinthians 3:11 — FOUNDATION

B. GOD CALLS MAN INTO PARTNERSHIP
   1. I Corinthians 3:9 — LABORERS WITH GOD
   2. John 20:21 — GOD SENDS MAN

C. MAN'S ROLE IN GOD'S PLAN
   1. I Corinthians 3:6 — PLANT
   2. I Corinthians 3:6 — CULTIVATE
   3. I Corinthians 3:6 — HARVEST

D. GOD'S ROLE IN THE LEADERSHIP TEAM
   1. I Corinthians 3:9 — HEAD
   2. Isaiah 6:8 — CALLS

***PRINCIPLE: Growing churches develop a leadership team with god at the head.***

## KEY #3:

*THE EARLY CHURCH DEVELOPED A SENSE OF COMMUNITY*

A. THE EARLY CHURCH MET IN HOUSE CHURCHES
   1. Acts 2:46 — MET DAILY IN ONE ACCORD
   2. Acts 5:42 — MET IN EVERY HOUSE TO TEACH & PREACH
   3. Acts 16:40 — MET IN LYDIA'S HOME
   4. I Corinthians 16:19 — MET IN ACQUILA AND PRISCILLA'S HOUSE

B. HOUSE CHURCH WORSHIP INGREDIENTS
   1. Acts 2:42 — TEACHING WORD
   2. Acts 2:42 — FELLOWSHIP
   3. Acts 2:42 — PRAYER
   4. Acts 2:42 — SHARING
   5. Acts 2:47 — PRAISE

C. SPIRITAL DYNAMICS OF HOUSE CHURCHES
1. MUTUAL SUPPORT TEAM
2. PERSONAL MINISTRY
3. KOINONIA FELLOWSHIP

*PRINCIPLE: Growing churches develop a sense of community that becomes the glue that binds the church together.*

## KEY #4:

*A SENSE OF COMMUNITY GAVE RISE TO OIKOS EVANGELISM*

A. THE GOSPEL TRAVELED IN FAMILY RELATIONSHIPS
1. John 1:40-41 — Andrew brought SIMON PETER
2. Luke 19:9 — Zacchaeus and his HOUSEHOLD
3. Acts 16:15 — Lydia and her HOUSEHOLD
4. Acts 16:33 — Phillippian jailer and his FAMILY

B. THE GOSPEL TRAVELED ALONG FRIENDSHIP LINES
1. Acts 10:24 Cornelius called together his kinsmen and NEAR FRIENDS to hear the gospel
2. John 4:39 Because of the testimony of the woman at the well, many SAMARITANS accepted Christ.
3. Mark 5:20 Jesus commanded the demoniac to go home and tell his FRIENDS WHAT GREAT THINGS He had done.
4. CONCLUSION: A Person's oikos includes FRIENDS NEIGHBORS RELATIVES WORK ASSOCIATES

*PRINCIPLE: Growing churches understand and employ the oikos principle of evangelism.*

## KEY #5:

*THE EARLY CHURCH DEVELOPED A GREAT COMMISSION STRATEGY*

Matthew 28:19-20 "go ye therefore, and teach all nations, baptizing them in the name of the Father, and of the Son, and of the Holy Ghost. Teaching them to observe all things whatsoever I have commanded you, and lo, I am with you always, even unto the end of the world."

A. FIVE ASPECTS OF THE GREAT COMMISSION
1. GOWING
2. SOWING
3. CULTIVATING
4. HARVESTING
5. DISCIPLING

B. THE INWARD FOCUS OF THE GREAT COMMISSION
1. CULTIVATING
2. DISCIPLING

C. THE OUTWARD FOCUS OF THE GREAT COMMISSION
1. GOING
2. SOWING
3. HARVESTING

*PRINCIPLE: Growing churches develop a balanced "great commission strategy".*

## KEY #6:

*THE EARLY CHURCH UNDERSTOOD AND EMPLOYED THE RECEPTIVITY PRINCIPLE OF CHURCH GROWTH*

Persons are more receptive to the gospel at various times in their lives.

A. BIBLICAL EXAMPLES OF RECEPTIVITY
1. Acts 16:25-32 — CRISIS / ACCEPTED CHRIST

2. Acts 26:28 — NORMAL / REJECTED CHRIST
3. Acts 8:26-39 — NORMAL / ACCEPTED CHRIST
4. Luke 23:42 — DEATH / ACCEPTED CHRIST

B. FOUR TYPES OF RESPONSES
   MATTHEW 13:1-9
   1. WAYSIDE — Matthew 13:4 fowls devoured the seed
   2. STONY — Matthew 13:5 sprung up with no root
   3. THORNY — Matthew 13:7 thorns choked the growing seeds
   4. GOOD — Matthew 13:8 brought forth much fruit

C. ALL HAD EXCUSES — LUKE 14:15-24
   Must look at ground I just bought
   Bought 5 yoke of oxen and must prove them
   Married a wife and cannot come

*PRINCIPLE: Growing churches understand and employ the "receptivity principle—find the people who are receptive.*

# KEY #7:

*THE EARLY CHURCH DEVELOPED AN EXCELLENT GROWTH CLIMATE*

A. UNITY
   1. Acts 2:46 — DOCTRINE IN ONE ACCORD
   2. Acts 2:46 — HAD THE SAME PURPOSE

B. AGAPE LOVE
   1. I John 3:14 — We know that we have passed from death unto life, because we love the brethren.
   2. LOVE BRINGS OUT THE BEST

C. EXPECTANCY
   1. POSITIVE ATTITUDE
   2. BELIEVED

D. COMMITMENT
   1. Acts 6:7 — OBEDIENT TO THE FAITH
   2. Acts 5:42 — CEASED NOT TO TEACH & PREACH JESUS CHRIST

*PRINCIPLE: Growing churches develop a conductive growth climate.*

# KEY #8:

*THE EARLY CHURCH ADOPTED THE MINISTRY MODEL OF JESUS*

A. THE MINISTRY MODEL OF JESUS
   1. Mark 10:46:52 — PHYSICAL NEEDS
   2. Matthew 14:15-21 — FOOD
   3. John 3:1-9 — SPIRITUAL NEEDS
   4. Matthew 25:31-46 — DOING FOR OTHERS

B. THE EARLY CHURCH DEVELOPED TOUCH MINISTRIES
   1. Acts 4:34-35 — SHARED POSSESSIONS
   2. Acts 31-11 — CONCERNED FOR PHYSICAL

3. Acts 2:47 — SPIRITUAL
4. Acts 6:1-3 — WIDOWS' NEEDS

C. OUR CHALLENGE
1. Matthew 9:36-39 — WORK IN HARVEST
2. Luke 6:19 — DEVELOPE TOUCH MINISTRIES

**FIND A NEED AND FILL IT!**

*PRINCIPLE: Churches grow as they build bridges to receptive persons by developing "touch ministries" that meet people's needs.*

## KEY #9:

*THE EARLY CHURCH USED A VARIETY OF RESOURCES*

A. THE EARLY CHURCH HAD A VARIETY OF RESOURCES
1. COMON LANGUAGE
2. EXCELLENT SYSTEM OF ROADS
3. THE GOSPEL
4. PEOPLE COMMITMENT TO GO AND TELL THE GOOD NEWS

B. THE EARLY CHURCH DEVELOPED TOUCH MINISTRIES
1. Acts 4:34-35 — SHARED POSSESSION
2. Acts 31-11 — CONCERNED FOR PHYSICAL
3. Acts 2:47 — SPIRITUAL
4. Acts 6:1-3 — WIDOWS' NEEDS

C. OUR CHALLENGE
1. Matthew 9:36-39 — WORK IN HARVEST
2. Luke 6:19 — DEVELOP TOUCH MINISTRIES

*PRINCIPLE: Growing churches use a variety of resources.*

## KEY #10:

*THE EARLY CHURCH USED VARIOUS METHODS IN THE DEVELOPMENT OF THEIR EVANGELISM STRATEGY*

A. EVANGELISTIC METHODS OF THE EARLY CHURCH
1. Acts 8:26-39 — PERSONAL WITNESSING
2. Acts 5:42 — TEACHING / PREACHING
3. Acts 13:1-3 — MISSIONARIES
4. Acts 2:41 — MASS MEETINGS
5. Romans 16:1-5 — HOUSE CHURCH
6. Acts 16:1-5 — CHURCH PLANTING

B. MODERN DAY EVANGELISTIC METHODS
1. revivals
2. personal evangelism
3. Small groups
4. media – radio / TV / newspaper
5. saturation evangelism
6. planting new churches
7. fellowship evangelism
8. Bible translation / tracts / music
9. Social Media
10. special events

*PRINCIPLE: Growing churches use a variety of evangelistic methods.*

# WHAT EVERY PASTOR NEEDS TO KNOW ABOUT MILLENNIALS

The average age of the modern (Protestant) pastor is 54, but millennials are those between the ages of 20 and 36. In 2017, they are the nation's largest living generation. In order to minister effectively to younger individuals, pastors should recognize these FOUR KEY FACTS ABOUT MILLENNIALS:

## 1. THEY INVEST IN THEIR CHILDREN.

Millennials came of age during times of financial difficulty in America.

- They are money-conscious. 67 percent of millennials stick to a budget, compared to 55 percent of Baby Boomers.
- The top 20 smartphone apps used by millennials are discount-focused.
- Nine out of ten millennials use coupons.
- Millennials may be hyper-focused on discounts, but there is one area where they outspend older generations: their children.
- Over half of millennials already have children, and they're more than willing to shell out their hard-earned dollars for high-quality children's products.
- They are 14 percent percent more likely than Baby Boomers to splurge for a groundbreaking new product.
- They are 39 percent more likely to check product labels for positive social and environmental effects.
- They will invest in sustainable, responsibly-made products, children's products in particular.
- **This tells pastors that millennials care about the quality of a church's children's program.** They want a positive environment for their children, and they're willing to part with something that's important to them (money) in order to achieve their goal.
- When churches prioritize children's programs, **millennials will take notice.**

## 2. THEY'RE TECHNOLOGICALLY SOCIAL.

- If a millennial hears about a local church that sparks their interest, you can bet their first step is to look up the church's official Facebook page to find out more.
- More than 85 percent of millennials own a smartphone.
- 86 percent of 18- to 29-year-olds use social media.
- In this case, the stereotype of the millennial glued to their phone is true, but this can work to the church's advantage.
- Use social media and smartphone technology to converse with your millennials.
- Share events on Facebook.
- Create a smartphone app that lists service times and streams the latest message.
- Modern technology and social networks are an opportunity for connection.

## 3. THEY WELCOME ONE-ON-ONE MENTORSHIP.

- According to the Barna Group, millennials who are connected with an older mentor are 59 percent more likely to stay in church.
- They don't shun advice from older generations —they welcome it.
- Millennials are looking for guidance. Is your church providing it?

## 4. THEY CRAVE AUTHENTICITY.

- Millennials don't care about the volume of the worship band or whether the pastor wears comfortable clothing.
- If they feel like a church is putting on a show to keep them in their seat, the seat will soon be vacant.
- There's a reason 84 percent of millennials don't trust traditional advertising. They can sense a counterfeit message a mile away.
- You don't have to put together a big production to entertain millennials—you just should

be real. According to David Kinnaman, president of the Barna Group, millennials are "not disillusioned with tradition; they are frustrated with slick or shallow expressions of religion."

- They want to be challenged intellectually.
- They want to see leaders be honest about everyday struggles.

## WHAT STRATEGIES DOES YOUR CHURCH USE TO REACH MILLENNIALS?

Permission to print
Contributed by partnersinministry.Org

# THINGS I HAVE LEARNED ALONG THE WAY

From the years of formal training, I can give you a lot of information I learned over the years. But there are things you learn from living, serving, and from practical experience that can never be taught in a classroom. In thinking back over 50+ years of ministry experience, several of these nuggets come to mind. I will share some that may be helpful to the reader.

## 1. YOU WILL NOT PLEASE EVERYONE ALL THE TIME.

*Galatians 1:10 (KJV)*
*For do I now persuade men, or God? or do I seek to please men? for if I yet pleased men, I should not be the servant of Christ.*

I was called to my first pastorate while I was a student at ECU and was 23 years old. I have always attended church but was not a leader nor a deacon. The church was a small country church. On a good Sunday we might have had 25-30 in attendance. Most of the adults were 50-85 years of age. My wife and I were the youngest couple in the church. There were two teenagers in the same family. No babies had been born in about 16 years.

I had many pleasant experiences. I visited in the homes of all the members. John Moore, Associational Missionary, who lived in Greenville, NC, mentored me and helped a lot. I learned the importance of getting to know your people. Since it was a small church, they had services only second and fourth Sunday mornings and Sunday school every Sunday.

They asked me to be their pastor. I had no experience—only willingness, availability, and a calling from the Lord to be a pastor. I had no experience in sermon preparation or delivery. They offered me $100 for preaching two Sundays per month.

I was a full-time student at ECU. Beth and I were married at age 19. Our first daughter, Rose, was born while I was a student and serving at this church. Rose was the first child born in the church in 16 years. Several families adopted us and Rose had numerous sets of grandparents. We really grew to love those people and they loved us.

Time came for the church to develop a new budget for the new church year. Many of the people wanted to give me a raise to show appreciation for the visiting and the job I had been doing as pastor. The budget committee met and decided to raise my salary from $50 per sermon to $75.

This taught me a valuable lesson. Everyone does not agree with everything. Some just look for an excuse to quit church.

## 2. GOD SHOWS UP WHEN YOU LEAST EXPECT HIM.

I pastored Stokes Baptist for two years. After I graduated from college I planned to move to Southeastern Seminary to continue my education. This incident happened the last winter I was pastor. One weekend, it started to snow on Saturday afternoon. Beth and I lived in Greenville, which was ten miles away. On Sunday morning, I called the deacon chairman and told him that, due to the weather, I was not planning on driving out for the service. I thought attendance would be lower than usual and I did not want to slide into the ditch. His response to me was, "Pastor please come." I could sense that he was expecting something unusual. Reluctantly I said, "OK I will come, but pray that I will not have a wreck or slide into the ditch."

I arrived safely. As the worship service began, people continued to come in. During my two years, I had been visiting three families whose husbands did not come to church. All three families, including the husbands, were in attendance. Weather was bad. But people continued to come in for worship. I do not remember what my message was that Sunday. But when God does a work in peoples' lives, the message is not that important as long as we lift up Jesus. After I finished the message, we began singing the invitation. On the first verse, one of the men stepped out and walked down the aisle and told me he wanted to be saved. I prayed with him and led him to pray the sinner's prayer. LORD, I know I am a sinner, I believe YOU are God's son, I believe YOU died on the cross for my sins, I believe YOU rose from the dead. Please come into my heart and save me from my sins and be my Savior.

*Acts 16:31 (KJV)*
*And they said, Believe on the Lord Jesus Christ, and thou shalt be saved.*

Before I finished praying with him, the second man stepped out and was in line for me to talk to him. He said, Pastor, please pray with me that God would save me."

Before I finished leading him to pray the sinner's prayer, the third man stepped out and was in line for me to talk to him.

I began talking to the third man and the third man prayed the sinner's prayer. Same thing. As he prayed, I sensed the small church was weeping and praising the Lord.

The church had been praying for these men for years. Their ages were 53, 65, and 73. Not too long after that Sunday, we had a baptism service. What a glorious and happy time that was. What a sight—the church probably had not had this many baptisms in several years. Chances are small that men this age will ever pray to be saved, especially three in one snowy service.

In thinking back about that snowy, cold Sunday, if we had called off the service, would they have come the following Sunday?

Maybe yes, maybe no. I praise God for that deacon encouraging me to come and not call off the service.

Matthew 18:20 (KJV)
For where two or three are gathered together in my name, there am I in the midst of them.

**THIS EXPERIENCE TAUGHT ME TO ALWAYS EXPECT GOD TO SHOW UP.**

### 3. MY CALL SHAPED MY MINISTRY.

I was born in Tarboro, NC, on my mother and father's wedding anniversary. My dad was serving in the Army during World War II.

My grandmother and grandfather took me home from the hospital. My mother could not assume the role of mother. I lived with my grandparents until the day Beth and I were married. I never lived with my mother. I remember her visiting me regularly. I never saw my dad until I was 20. My mother had a lot of problems. She had a serious drinking problem and was an alcoholic. By the time I was 15, Mom had been married four times. She never was a factor or influence in my life.

*Romans 8:28 (KJV)*
*And we know that all things work together for good to them that love God, to them who are the called according to his purpose.*

I learned that God uses everything to help us develop spiritually. The bad and the good work together.

I have always gone to church. I grew up going to FBC, Tarboro. When I was nine, I accepted Jesus as my Savior. I was baptized shortly afterward. When I was 15, a missionary came to our church who was serving in South America. He showed slides of his work. The last slide was a picture of a jungle sunset. He talked about how many lost people there are in the world. God needs people willing to answer the call to go and tell the Gospel story that JESUS SAVES. He quoted from Isaiah 6:8 (KJV): "Also I heard the voice of the Lord, saying, Whom shall I send, and who will go for us? Then said I, Here am I; send me."

At the invitation, he said God might be calling someone here tonight. My heart felt as if it were pounding out of my chest. I felt that God was speaking to me. What could I do? I was so young! I walked down the aisle and took my pastor by the hand and I told him that I felt God was speaking to me. To this day, I can still see that picture 60 years later. The pastor prayed for me and asked that I come by to talk with him.

During this conversation, he explained what came next. He said college and seminary were seven years. That really scared me. School was OK but was not where I really wanted to be. (Earning my bachelor's, master's, and doctorate took 12 years.)

Most Baptist churches had Training Union on Sunday nights prior to the worship service. My youth leaders were Bobby and Gail Cross. They asked me to develop a talk and they would let me stand up before the class and give it. I thought about it and reluctantly agreed. My pastor, Joe Larrimore, let me use his commentaries. I did a study on John 14:6 (KJV): "Jesus saith unto him, I am the way, the truth, and the life: no man cometh unto the Father, but by me."

After my presentation, everyone seemed to be really excited. In a few days my pastor asked me if I would give my talk on Sunday night at church. I reluctantly said yes. After my presentation, some of the people began telling me that God had his hand on me and had something special for me to do with my life. The church people affirmed what I thought in my heart—God had called me into ministry.

*"For many are called, but few are chosen"* (Matthew 22:14, KJV) . I never heard the voice of God; however, I knew without a doubt God called me. People from two churches affirmed it. I did not choose to be a minister but God chose me.

*John 15:16 (KJV)*
*Ye have not chosen me, but I have chosen you, and ordained you, that ye should go and bring forth fruit, and that your fruit should remain: that whatsoever ye shall ask of the Father in my name, he may give it you.*

Word spread and soon I received several invitations to speak at other churches. God just blessed the message and me each time I gave it. Soon I met the girl of my dreams and I started going to church with her at West Edgecombe Baptist Church. By this time, I was in grade 11. In a few months, WEBC wanted to have YOUTH SUNDAY. To this day, I do not know how it happened.

One of the deacons asked me if I would be the main speaker. WHY ME, LORD? I said yes. God really blessed and people in West Edgecombe began telling me the same thing the people in Tarboro had told me. They felt that God had something special for me to do and they felt HE was calling me into the ministry. Down deep inside, I knew and felt the same thing. I had many questions. How would I pay for school? How did Beth feel about my calling? I was not a minister when we began dating. She was the person I wanted to share all of my life with.

WEBC licensed me into the Gospel Ministry in 1965. Beth and I moved to Greenville and I started college at ECU.

WHERE WOULD THE MONEY COME FROM? GOD ALWAYS SHOWED UP. MY AUNT PAID ALL MY TUITION WHILE AT ECU. MY FOUR-YEAR EDUCATION WAS $1,400. I graduated in 33 months and debt free, in preparation for attending Southeastern Baptist Theological Seminary in Wake Forest. During our time at ECU, our first child Rose was born.

## 4. MY FIRST GOSPEL PRESENTATION.

To be honest, I had never presented the Gospel to anyone. I was now the pastor of a church and did not know how. My mother and stepfather lived in Denver, CO. I really had a burden to witness to her. The problem I had was the two weeks between summer school and fall quarter. I was obligated to attend summer camp as I was in the Army Reserve. I prayed, "Lord, please make it possible for me to travel to Denver and witness to my mother." My wife had some vacation time, but serving on active duty for two weeks stood in my way. I prayed and prayed and prayed some more. One day I came home for lunch. The mailman came and I had a letter from the US Army. The letter stated that I would not have to attend the two weeks active duty. I jumped for joy. I called Beth at work and told her a MIRACLE happened. She could not believe it. We immediately began making plans to head for DENVER.

I learned a valuable lesson. WHEN GOD IS IN SOMETHING, THE US ARMY CAN NOT STOP IT. Denver was about 2,000 miles from Greenville, NC. I called MOM and told her we were coming. We needed to make sure they would be home. They said to come on, that they would be waiting for us.

My main purpose of going was to tell her how to be saved. We loaded up and headed for Denver. It took three long days of traveling to get there.

We arrived on Sunday and planned to come home the next Sunday. It was good to visit with MOM and my third step-father (her fourth husband). On Monday, I procrastinated witnessing to her until Tuesday. When Tuesday came, I put it off until Wednesday. When Saturday came, I knew that must be the day because we were leaving on Sunday to return to NC. It is really difficult to witness to your mom, especially when you have not witnessed to anyone before. I prayed for God to give me an extra portion of HIS strength.

I did not know the Roman Road or any plan of salvation. But I did know this verse:

*"And they said, Believe on the Lord Jesus Christ, and thou shalt be saved, and thy house" (Acts 16:31-32, KJV).*

My mom and stepfather were sitting with us in the living room. I said, "MOM, I want to share something with you." She said, "Son, go ahead." I told her how Jesus had come into my life and saved me when I was nine years old. And that I knew without a doubt that if I died, I would go to heaven. I asked her, "Mom, have you ever accepted Christ?" I never will forget her response. "Son, do you think God will save me from my sins?" She was an alcoholic and had several men in her life. I responded by saying, "I know He will." I asked her if she would like to pray with me to ask Jesus to come into her heart. She said, "I sure do." I looked over to my stepfather and noticed his tears were flowing. I asked him if he would like to pray to receive Christ. He said he sure would. My mother and stepfather both prayed with me that Jesus would come into their hearts and forgive them of their sins.

WOW, what an experience. I could hear the angels rejoicing. "Likewise, I say unto you, there is joy in the presence of the angels of God over one sinner that repenteth" (Luke 15:10, KJV). Joy in heaven when one repents, and twice as much joy with two repenting. A few months later, my mom and stepfather came to visit us in NC.

**MY MOM AND STEPDAD WERE THE FIRST TWO PEOPLE I EVER LED TO THE LORD AND BAPTIZED AS A MINISTER.**

## 5. BEHIND EVERY GOOD MINISTER IS A GOOD WIFE.

I am convinced that Beth is the best wife any man could ever have. We met when we were in the eleventh grade. We dated several years and married in 1962, when we were 19 years old—55 years ago. She has been a wonderful companion, wife, pastor's wife, mother to our two children, and grandmother to our two grandsons. When I think of her, I think of these following passages:

> *Proverbs 31:10 (KJV)*
> *Who can find a virtuous woman? for her price is far above rubies.*
>
> *Proverbs 31:29-30 (KJV)*
> *Many daughters have done virtuously, but thou excellest them all. Favour is deceitful, and beauty is vain: but a woman that feareth the LORD, she shall be praised.*

### A FEW COMMENTS ABOUT BETH:
- She was saved at an early age and has loved the Lord all her life.
- We had similar backgrounds—she was raised by her aunt and uncle and I was raised by my grandparents.
- We both have always been in church.
- She has always been very supportive and my companion.
- She has been willing to do whatever.
- WE LEARNED THAT GOD WILL TAKE CARE OF US.

### FOR MANY YEARS WE HAVE LIVED ON THE EDGE:
- When I graduated from college, we resigned our jobs to move to Wake Forest.
- Instead of moving to Wake Forest we moved to Maysville where I served as pastor for 19 months.

- After two years we moved to Wake Forest from Maysville to move closer to school.
- In a few months, we moved to Oak City.
- In four years, we moved from Oak City to Durham where I served as associate minister. I worked primarily with youth and children.
- We moved from Durham to Rocky Mount, where we have lived for 40 years. I first served as pastor of Oakdale Baptist Church for 8 years.
- I resigned from Oakdale to begin a freelance ministry of planning camps, writing, and teaching seminars.

## SOME EVENTS REQUIRED AN EXTRA PORTION OF FAITH AND GRACE:

- The Foreign Mission Board asked me to go to South Africa to teach church growth conferences to the missionaries and South African pastors.
- We set a budget and raised $10,000 for the two-month trip in 1989. GOD PROVIDED THE FUNDS.
- When I resigned Oakdale in 1985 we had no jobs or salary. GOD PROVIDED.
- Many ministry opportunities were provided. We never LACKED or went hungry.
- WHERE GOD GUIDES HE PROVIDES.

## MY WRITING EXPERIENCE

*UNLOCKING YOUR CHURCH GROWTH POTENTIAL DISSERTATION AT FULLER THEOLOGICAL SEMINARY*

For my doctoral dissertation, after consulting with my major professor, C. Peter Wagner, I researched why 90 percent of churches were not growing. I proposed how to recognize the obstacles and barriers and how to overcome them. I sold 2,000 copies and made enough to pay the tuition for my degree. Total sales of 5,000 copies of *Unlocking Your Church Growth Potential.*

## BREAKING BARRIERS OF NEW CHURCH GROWTH

I was asked by the Southern Baptist Home Mission Board Church Extension Department to develop a book from information I would gather from all the church planters supported by the HMB. Questionnaires were mailed to 1,000 church planters across the US. I compiled the results in this book. From this data gathered, I identified the 35, 75, and 125 attendance barriers. I located a book printer and eventually did two printings. Total sales of 10,000 copies. I had income from my book sales.

## DISTRIBUTION OF BREAKING BARRIERS:

- The HMB bought 2,000 copies and distributed to all the church planters in the US.
- I contacted all the Baptist mission directors in each SBC convention state. Most ordered multiple copies.
- I contacted the Baptist Book Stores (Lifeway). About 40 bookstores stocked my book.
- Eleven colleges and seminaries used the book as a text in church growth/church planting.
- Sold most of the 10,000 copies printed all over the US. Distributed some in South Africa while on a mission trip teaching South African pastors church growth principles.
- Donated 100+ copies to the Appalachian Regional Ministry, Bill Barker, director, to distribute to the pastors in Appalachia.

## EVANGELISM TOOLS FOR THE 90S

This book included a variety of ideas on reaching the harvest. Rick Warren contributed a chapter—Reaching Baby Boomers. Tom Cheyney contributed a chapter using the Telecomputer.

## CHURCH GROWTH PROFILE

While studying at Fuller and after graduation, I developed a Church Growth Profile. This tool was designed to reveal obstacles and barriers and assist in growth planning.

## PURPOSE:

- To lead a church to understand their growth dynamics and growth patterns.
- To lead a church to analyze their obstacles and barriers.

- To develop a plan that would promote growth.

## PROCEDURE:

- Study 20-year growth trends—attendance, baptisms, offerings, mission giving, new members.
- Distribute church questionnaire—determine average age, length of membership, and living patterns.
- Ask questions relating to general health of the church.
- What one thing would you like to see your church do differently?
- What advice do you have for the pastor?

## DEMOGRAPHIC STUDY –

- Most Baptist Associations and Methodist Conferences can obtain this info without cost to the church.
- I like to include a three- and five-mile radius from the church. This will give you ages in the community, population, education level, average income.
- Interview church members—select all ages. If church has 100 active members, interview 15-20. Ask questions like,"What is the greatest thing that has happened during the past five years? What would you like to see your church do during the next five years?"
- The Written Report: After gathering the data, distributing the questionnaire, studying demographics, and interviewing the members, I would prepare a written report. The written report includes the summary of everything.
- Recommendations: I always presented my report to the church along with five or six recommendations based upon my findings.
- Time requirements: Usually takes 10-12 weeks from start to finish.

## RESULTS OF DOING THE CHURCH PROFILE:

Many factors resulted. Like going to the doctor with a weight problem. He can tell us what to do and how to lose weight. The problem is getting motivated to take action. I am happy to say several churches took my recommendations seriously and did quite well. These churches had a remarkable turnaround and experienced tremendous growth. Other churches put the Growth Profile Report on the shelf or in the drawer and did nothing with it.

## YOUTH ON MISSION, 1992-2009

Teaching church growth conferences/ church planter conferences in 35 states and on the national level at Ridgecrest was a great benefit. I gained many insights into the practical aspects of church growth. I had the greatest experiences teaching, talking to, and learning from many church planters who were on the field working, trying to grow their church. I met many of these people and I saw their struggles, hopes, and dreams. I developed a dream. Suppose I could develop an organization that could assist churches?

Youth On Mission's first mission trip was in the Baltimore/Washington area. I had met state mission directors in both the MD/DE and Washington, DC Baptist Conventions while teaching conferences around the country. In addition, I became acquainted with the leaders of the Salvation Army and Soup Kitchens. I had met the Director of the Free Methodist Conference, as I had taught a conference in their conference center/camp. It would house 150 people and had a kitchen were we could do our cooking. I spread the word around and seven churches wanted to take the first mission trip with me.

Our missions in the DC/BLT area: The Inner Harbor Ministry in Baltimore, soup kitchen, several churches, the Salvation Army and the Soup Kitchen in DC.

- I employed the cooks.
- I reserved the camp. I planned the recreation —touring DC, attending Orioles baseball game, and other special sites.

YOM was one of the first turn-key mission experiences in the US, meaning we planned mission assignments, lodging, nightly worship, meals, and staff.

## INNER CITY SITES INCLUDE:

| | |
|---|---|
| Honolulu | Los Angeles |
| San Francisco | San Diego |
| Denver | El Paso |
| Dallas | New Orleans |
| St. Louis | Idaho Falls, IA |
| Chicago | Buffalo |
| Philadelphia | Baltimore |
| Washington | Atlanta |
| Orlando | Miami |
| Morehead City, NC | |

## APPALACHIAN AREA:

| | |
|---|---|
| WEST VIRGINIA | KENTUCKY |
| Charleston | Pikeville |
| Huntington | Lexington |
| Huntersville | Ashland |
| Buchannan | NC |
| VIRGINIA | Asheville |
| Jonesville | |
| Bluefield | |

## CANADA:

Toronto, Ontario Hamilton, Ontario Calgary, Alberta

**CONCLUSION: NAMB**, the North American Mission Board of the Southern Baptist Convention, honored me with a plaque for recruiting 50,000 volunteer missionaries. This was a feat no one else in the United States had ever done. I give God all the glory for reaching this milestone.

Since receiving the plaque, numbers have reached 60,000. Also, YOM was instrumental in providing the model for New Orleans Baptist Seminary's MISSION LAB.

**I BELIEVE EACH MINISTRY OPPORTUNITY PREPARED ME FOR THE NEXT ONE. TO GOD BE THE GLORY.**

---

**Continuing to Leap**
Keeping the Faith 2017
*Not Equal Gifts, but Equal Sacrifice*

**SOUTHSIDE BAPTIST CHURCH**
Rocky Mount, NC

To help provide funds for our new building, we intend to give
$ _____ weekly for 156 weeks for a total of $ _____
$ _____ monthly for 36 months for a total of $ _____
Or as follows _____
Beginning _____
This statement of intention may be revised or cancelled

Name _____ phone _____
Address _____ email _____
Signature _____

**THE CONTINUING-TO-LEAP CAMPAIGN PURPOSE: MARCH 5, 2017, the fifth anniversary on hwy 97:**

1. PAY OFF AS MUCH OF THE EXISTING LOAN ($500,000) AS POSSIBLE.
2. PHASE II: GET IN A POSITION TO BUILD PHASE II – THE FAMILY LIFE CENTER.

**UPDATE:**
IN A BUSINESS MEETING IN APRIL 2017, SOUTHSIDE CALLED REV. C.J. CAUBLE AS SENIOR PASTOR. HE SERVED AS ASSOCIATE PASTOR WITH DR. FOWLER FOR FOUR AND A HALF YEARS. AND THE STORY CONTINUES.

# CONCLUSIONS

**IT HAS BEEN A JOY WRITING THIS BOOK AND TELLING THE SOUTHSIDE STORY.** I pray the book will be an inspiration to you and help you in your ministry.

It has been a great joy serving as pastor these seven YEARS, 2009-2016. I was 66 years old at the beginning, and almost 74 when I retired.

I have been asked many times what the key was to our success. This is not a simple one-word answer but I will give it a try.

**WHY HAS SOUTHSIDE GROWN AND OTHER CHURCHES DECLINED?**
- PEOPLE had a mind to work.
- Staying on Church Street would have meant sure death and the people realized it.
- They did not want their church to die.
- The leadership followed the pastor.
- The people were a giving people.
- It was in God's timing.
- HOW IMPORTANT WAS I TO THE GROWTH?
- I had a variety of experiences in church growth, evangelism, church planting, and pastoring.
- People tell me my strength is my people skills.
- I LOVED THE LORD.
- I LOVED THE PEOPLE.

**SUMMARY:**
*I WAS THE RIGHT PERSON, IN THE RIGHT PLACE, AT THE RIGHT TIME, AND GOD USED ME TO LEAD THE PEOPLE.*

**WE ALL TOOK A LEAP OF FAITH.**
We believed that:
- God would lead us.
- God would honor our faith.
- God would provide.

---

The Bible never once says, "figure it out." But over and over it says, "trust God."

He's already got it all figured out.

---

**MY ENCOURAGEMENT TO YOU MY READER:**
1. STUDY the principles in this book.
2. Study the DEMOGRAPHICS.
3. Do the GROWTH PROFILE.
4. INTERVIEW the people.
5. ANALYZE your barriers.
6. INCREASE your entrance points.
7. PLAN OUTREACH EVENTS.
8. INVOLVE people in OUTREACH MINISTRIES.
9. PLAN ADVERTISING.
10. TAKE THE LEAP OF FAITH—both pastor and people.
11. RETIREMENT is not in the BIBLE.

www.ingramcontent.com/pod-product-compliance
Lightning Source LLC
Chambersburg PA
CBHW081337080526
44588CB00017B/2648